KEY CONTROLS:
THE SOLUTION FOR
SARBANES-OXLEY
INTERNAL CONTROL
COMPLIANCE

by
James Brady Vorhies, CIA, CISA, CPA

The IIA Research
Foundation

ISBN 0-89413-529-5
04055   03/04
First Printing

DEDICATION

This book is dedicated to Biggs C. Porter,
W. Randall Stewart,
and David H. Anderson.

CONTENTS

ABOUT THE AUTHOR

James Brady Vorhies, CIA, CISA, CPA, has a bachelor of arts degree in economics from The University of Texas. He also has an MBA in finance and a master of science degree in accounting from The University of North Texas.

He has extensive internal audit experience for several firms and is a Certified Internal Auditor, a Certified Information Systems Auditor, and a Certified Public Accountant. In his risk monitoring role, James reports directly to the corporate controller of a Fortune 500 firm while also working extensively with the firm's chief audit executive.

Over two years ago, James designed and implemented a key controls process for the firm's accounting functions. In addition to the ongoing key controls processes, James manages the quarterly review of his firm's disclosure controls and procedures and the U.S. Sarbanes-Oxley Act of 2002 Sections 302 and 906 certification supporting processes. James is also responsible for several key roles in developing his firm's Sarbanes-Oxley Section 404 process among which are designing and implementing the overall business process and supporting automated and manual systems.

ACKNOWLEDGMENTS

All of the opinions expressed in this book are those of the author and the author alone. The author has attempted to acknowledge all sources and persons holding copyright or reproduction rights for passages quoted and for illustrations reproduced in this book, especially:

How Fraud Hurts You and Your Organization, training course sponsored by the American Institute of Certified Public Accountants (AICPA) and the Association of Certified Fraud Examiners (ACFE).

The *Public Company Accounting Reform and Investor Protection Act of 2002*, commonly known as the Sarbanes-Oxley Act.

Securities and Exchange Commission *Final Rule: Certifications and Disclosures In Companies' Annual Reports*, dated August 29, 2002, release number 33-8124.

Securities and Exchange Commission *Proposed Rule: Disclosure Required by Sections 404, 406 and 407 of the Sarbanes-Oxley Act of 2002*, dated October 22, 2002, release number 33-8138.

AICPA Auditing Standard Board's Exposure Draft *Proposed Statements on Auditing Standards Auditing an Entity's Internal Control Over Financial Reporting in Conjunction With the Financial Statement Audit and Amendment to Statement on Auditing Standards No. 100, Interim Financial Information, Proposed Statement on Standards for Attestation Engagements Reporting on an Entity's Internal Control Over Financial Reporting*, dated March 18, 2003.

PCAOB Public Company Accounting Oversight Board's *Proposed Auditing Standard – An Audit of Internal Control Over Financial Reporting Performed In Conjunction With an Audit of Financial Statements*, PCAOB Release No. 2003-17, October 7, 2003.

Protivit's *Guide to the Sarbanes-Oxley Act: Internal Control Reporting Requirements Frequently Asked Questions Regarding Section 404*.

Lord Bissell Brook *Client Alert Sarbanes-Oxley Act of 2002*.

Section 404 of the Sarbanes-Oxley Act: A Practice Guide, PricewaterhouseCoopers, March 2003.

Statement of Financial Accounting Standards No. 5 *Accounting for Contingencies*.

Committee of Sponsoring Organizations of the Treadway Commission (COSO), *Internal Control – Integrated Framework*, September 1992. Also, the COSO Web site at www.coso.org.

Control Objectives for Information and related Technology, CobiT 3rd Edition by the Information Systems Audit and Control Foundation (ISACF) in 1996.

Jefferson Wells International for allowing the usage of their graphic of a COSO cube.

FASB Statement No. 5, Accounting for Contingencies.

INTRODUCTION

Anyone who is intending to read this book will have heard of the U.S. Sarbanes-Oxley Act of 2002. This act is the most sweeping legislation and set of enhancements to the securities laws since the original Exchange Acts were passed back in 1933 and 1934. Among the Sarbanes-Oxley Act's 1107 sections are the amendments in Sections 404 and 302. Section 404 requires public companies to perform an annual evaluation of their internal control processes.

These companies are also required to publish an annual report on this evaluation. The company's external audit firm is required to report on and attest to management's assertions regarding their internal control processes as published in their annual report(s). Proposed enhancements to the current Section 302 quarterly certifications will require these same companies to evaluate their internal control processes quarterly beginning in 2004. Most of you will be motivated to develop a key controls process because of these Section 404 and 302 requirements.

You are probably interested in what this book can teach you about a key controls process because you are concerned about the cost of audit findings and issues that, if they occur, your company will have to disclose in your company's annual report and the impact that these disclosures can have on your company's stock price. Or perhaps you are concerned about the high cost of the annual audit of internal controls that your external auditors will perform and you want to know how you can minimize these costs. Or you may be concerned about the resources that are needed to develop an adequate internal control review process to comply with Sections 404 and 302 requirements and want to maximize the company's benefit from developing such a system. And, if you are not worried about these issues, I will explain why you should be. I will also explain why the development of a key controls process is your best solution to address these risks, to minimize these costs, and to maximize the benefit from your investment.

However, as important as the need to implement an evaluation system that will facilitate compliance with Sarbanes-Oxley Act requirements is, this still is not the most important or compelling reason to implement a key controls process. The most compelling reason to understand the key controls process and to implement it in your company is because it is good management practice. Management has a need to know that the right things are being done right, which means in an accurate, complete, and timely manner. It is a process that enables management to achieve this objective. It is an ongoing self-audit process based on quality control and assurance principles. It is a process that identifies both control weaknesses within existing internal control processes and an ongoing risk assessment process, which identifies and communicates new risks as they occur. And, it is a process that both ensures and gives assurance that all significant control weaknesses and risks will be identified and reported timely along with a proposed solution, a resolution time line, and an assessment of the potential financial impact to the appropriate level of management in order to ensure that there is adequate visibility, resource allocation, accountability, and timely risk mitigation.

Anyone reading this book will probably know that the control objectives of management are timeless while the control activities employed change over time as processes evolve due to changes in technology and other control environmental effects and requirements. This forces management to constantly struggle to develop a process of internal control that can achieve its control objectives at minimal cost. Key controls processes are an internal controls evaluation and exception control process. And, yes, almost everyone now needs a process like this because of the Sarbanes-Oxley Act. However, as always there are an almost endless number of different control processes that can be developed. Therefore, the processes described in this book may not fit every company exactly. However, the lessons learned and all of the information provided will help to ensure that you can understand how a key controls process can best help your company, and how best to design such a process for your company. Finally, once you have read this book I am convinced that you will not only understand why the development of a key controls process is a good management practice, but why it should be a best practice.

Although this is a somewhat technical subject, I know that readers with very diverse backgrounds and knowledge levels related to internal control will attempt to read this book. For that reason, I have in Chapter 1 attempted to provide the reader with a basic understanding of internal control. Readers with an advanced understanding may want to skip this chapter or they might find it a welcome refresher. In Chapter 2, I give the reader a thorough explanation of the requirements and the risks inherent in the new Sarbanes-Oxley Act Sections 404, 302, and 906, and explain why the key controls process is the best process to assist you in complying with these requirements.

Next, I walk the reader through a complete coverage of the subject. This includes detailed explanations of all of the key controls process' concepts, components, and subprocesses with examples to enable the reader to understand these concepts. This coverage builds upon itself as one advances through the book. Therefore, a concept described at some depth in Chapter 2 may be explained again in much greater depth so as to give the reader a much more thorough knowledge in Chapter 11. I encourage the reader to read the entire book at least once in order to be able to see how all of the key controls process' elements are developed and work together.

My hope is that this book will provide the guidance necessary to enable you to understand how to build the most efficient and effective key controls process for your company.

CHAPTER SUMMARY

An overview of the contents of each chapter follows:

Chapter 1: Internal Control

An overview of internal control — what it is and what it is not; why it is important; and just about everything you should know about it. This chapter is intended to quickly bring the internal control novice up to speed so that they can understand the rest of the book. It provides the COSO definition of internal control and gives the reader the option to skip the chapter if he or she already understands the definition.

Chapter 2: Why You Need a Key Controls Process

This chapter explains the Sarbanes-Oxley Act requirements, including disclosure controls and procedures; internal control over financial reporting; what a key controls process is; and the 10 best reasons why you should develop one.

Chapter 3: The Key Controls Process

The key controls process is explained in detail from a theoretical basis, including how the process should be designed so that it will be an ongoing self-audit, quality control, risk assessment, and reporting process that will both ensure and give assurance that the right things are being done right.

Chapter 4: Developing Key Controls

This chapter explains a step-by-step process for performing a successful internal control review. This includes how to review the adequacy of the design of internal controls and the identification of control gaps, how to test internal controls, and, most importantly, how to identify your key controls.

Chapter 5: The Minimum Standard of Control

This chapter explains the concept of "minimum standards of control" and why they are critical to developing an ongoing internal control quality control process. Also explained is the equally important concept of "frequency of review."

Chapter 6: The Key Controls Verification and Exception Reporting Process

The chapter explains the criteria that must be present to ensure that key control exceptions are not just identified and reported, but are appropriately mitigated.

Chapter 7: The Significant Events and Judgments Reporting Process

While key controls are defined quality control points that are established and reviewed against established quality control standards for an existing process, environmental risks must also be identified, assessed, and managed. This chapter explains how one should identify and communicate these significant events and judgments up through the management ranks to ensure that there is an appropriate risk management process integrated into the overall key controls process.

Chapter 8: The Key Controls and Significant Events and Judgments Certification Process

This chapter explains the different levels of management certifications necessary to ensure appropriate review and approval without duplication of effort. Also explained are the types of certification statements that should be made related to the identification and reporting of internal control design and operating deficiencies, fraud, the fair presentation of financial results, and other required disclosures.

Chapter 9: Key Controls and COSO's Internal Control Framework

This chapter explains the COSO internal control framework and the Sarbanes-Oxley Act Section 404 requirements for adopting such a framework. Also explained is how the key controls and significant events and judgments reporting and certification process fits within this framework.

Chapter 10: Key Controls and Enterprise Risk Assessment and Management

The chapter explains how a key controls and significant events and judgments reporting and certification process integrates into and supports an overall enterprise risk assessment and management process.

Chapter 11: Key Controls and Disclosure Controls and Procedures

Disclosure controls and procedures and other Sarbanes-Oxley Act Section 302 requirements are explained in detail, along with a best practice approach for developing disclosure controls and procedures and integrating these effectively with a key controls process.

Chapter 12: Developing a Key Controls System

The types of automated systems currently available to assist in automating a key controls process are discussed. The specifications for a fully integrated customized key controls and risk assessment and management system are also defined.

Chapter 13: Negative Competition

A new theory for understanding internal control failure is defined and explained. These negative competitive practices are defined in hopes of enabling future auditors to begin to be able to understand, identify, and control these practices.

Chapter 14: Key Controls Integrated Framework

This final chapter puts all of the pieces together and explains how to develop a fully integrated key controls process.

CHAPTER 1
INTERNAL CONTROL

> **"Trust in God. Audit everyone else."**
> **— Anonymous**

If you are an expert in internal control, you may want to skip this chapter. However, since my goal is to enable almost anyone to be able to read and profit from this book, this first chapter will help develop a basis understanding of internal control for those who need it. As a test, you might want to jump to the chapter summary and read the Committee of Sponsoring Organizations of the Treadway Commission's (COSO) definition of internal control. If you understand the definition, proceed to Chapter 2. If you need a little assistance, please continue reading.

The Need for Control

Before we can explain what key controls are, we will need to begin with the concept of internal control. Since the very beginning of time, and probably the very first time someone convinced someone else to do something for him or her, mankind has struggled with the question, "How do I let someone else do it and still get it done my way?" And with this one question and natural desire, control as an issue was born. It is really that simple. We all want it done our way even if someone else is doing it for us, and we get especially sensitive when it comes to others handling our money. And, in the business world, everything is related to money. As you add more and more people who are performing tasks for you the question becomes, "How do I ensure that they are doing things like I want?" To make this task even more difficult (as you probably know), once you have added enough people, you go from being their friend to becoming management. I'm not sure how this transformation takes place, and I believe that I will leave it for someone else to explain.

Let's imagine that we are the management of a small pizza parlor, and we want to ensure that the right things get done the right way. To enable this to happen, we first have to determine what the right way is, because as we all know, if *we* don't know the right way it is difficult to tell anyone else. Once we have determined the right way to do things, in order to effectively and efficiently communicate these requirements to our employees we need to proceduralize this process. In other words, we develop specific steps and expectations. Then, we develop a policy — written, of course. If we simply have our employees read this policy, we should be able to sleep soundly at night knowing that everyone is going to do what we want just the way we want it to be done, right? Well, the problem is that in any business process there are inherent risks that the right things will not get done right. These inherent risks of errors, mistakes, and even fraud — which, if not appropriately controlled, can lead to public embarrassment, financial losses, bankruptcy, and even prison time — drive management to want to control and limit or eliminate these risks.

Therefore, because of the inherent risks that exist in any business process, management has an inherent objective to control these risks. These objectives are called **"control objectives."** Now, as management we have many objectives; and as much as we may or may not like it, we have many limitations. We realize that we cannot get it exactly like we want it. We need to allow for employee individualism, diversity, and creativity, but we still want to ensure that the work is done in a manner that is appropriately authorized, accurate, efficient, and complete. The alternative is that the work is performed in an unauthorized or haphazard manner, where it is inaccurate, inefficient, and incomplete. These are just some of management's control objectives for a normal business process.

Control Objectives

Let's explore management's control objectives because, as driven by the risks of failure, these objectives are what cause the need for internal control. Following is a list of typical financial control objectives, along with a detailed explanation of each:

Authorization

Management authorizes transactions. After all, you do not want your employees giving away your money without your permission. So you start off running the till and you probably pay all of the bills. However, eventually you decide to trust someone else to pay the bills, but you still insist that you sign all of the checks and that yours is the only authorized signature on the bank account. This enables you to trust — appropriately — that you will authorize and control all disbursements.

Accuracy

Transactions are appropriately calculated. You don't want your employees paying too much or too little. The same goes for the size of the pizzas they serve. Too much and you are giving away your profits; too little and you can anger your customers. In fact, just being inconsistent between customers in relation to how much pizza sauce or toppings you serve each one can upset them. This is where the tie-in between control and quality comes into play. We will discuss this more later, but for now let's agree that when it comes to quality, what we are really trying to achieve is a consistent level.

Completeness

All valid transactions are recorded. As management, how would you feel if your cashier only recorded the transactions that he or she wanted to record? A few years ago, I was leaving a major metropolitan airport after having left my car in long-term parking for several days. When I drove up to the cashier's booth, the attendant took my ticket and calculated the amount I owed without entering it into his cash register. Then, he told me how much I owed and asked me if I needed a receipt. I was incensed because it was obvious to me that he fully intended to pocket my money and never record the transaction in the cash register — if I did not need a receipt. Needless to say, I demanded a receipt. I also felt like calling up his boss and informing him that he had a weakness in his control process because it was possible for his employees to not record valid transactions without his knowing.

Existence

Recorded transactions actually occurred and were recorded only once. Here the objective is to (a) only pay bills that you actually owe, and (b) only pay each bill once. In current payables processing operations two of the primary objectives are to ensure that the vendor/payee is valid (i.e., that someone is not pretending to be a vendor so that you pay them for goods and services you never actually received) and that duplicate payments do not occur, or are found and appropriate refunds are received if duplicate payments have occurred.

Valuation

Appropriate measurement and recognition principles applied. Here is where we first begin to get into **"accounting."** Obviously, the management of our pizza parlor wants its business accounted for correctly. In order to do so, you must be able to ensure that you value sales and costs correctly. Most pizza parlors do not have a problem with this. Obviously you record a sale when it occurs in the amount owed and you have both recognized and measured the amount of revenue correctly. However, this is actually an area in which many companies get into trouble. In fact, many of the recent frauds were actually related to valuation. The drive to improve short-term profits sometimes causes management to recognize revenues before they are actually earned, and should be recognized. Sometimes management will delay the recognition of expenses that should be recorded in the current period.

These seem to be simple issues; however, valuation is actually very difficult. For example, let's assume you have been expanding your pizza business and earlier this year you purchased land. You also built a plant on this land to make pizza crusts and to prepare the sauce and other pizza ingredients for the pizza parlors in this new sales area. In addition, you built several new pizza parlors earlier in the year. But, as soon as you complete the factory and pizza parlors, there is an economic downturn that causes tough competition. Near the end of the year, you end up closing several of the pizza parlors in this sales area. Due to the closure of these parlors, the new crust and ingredient factory is **"impaired."** The factory is impaired because the plant was built to support an expanding market and over 50 new pizza parlors in this sales area. However, only 20 new parlors were built, and now 10 of them are closed. Further, it is clear that new pizza parlors will not be built in this sales area until the economy improves. Due to the tough competition, new pizza parlors may never be built. It is possible that all 10 of the existing parlors will be closed if their profitability does not improve.

Now, as management, you have been able to grow your business over the last several years and your stock is traded on the New York Stock Exchange. As a publicly traded company, you have a responsibility to value your assets correctly, to report your past earnings correctly, and to fully disclose any information necessary so that both stock and debt holders for your company can appropriately understand the future economic prospects and earnings capability of your company. At the same time, you have short-term earnings pressures and recognize that if you do not return an appropriate rate-of-return on invested capital, your company's stock price may plummet and you will have difficulty raising additional capital and debt necessary to grow the business.

From a valuation perspective you realize that you have invested over $5 million in the crust and ingredients factory, which is only operating at 20 percent of capacity. And, the factory is not currently worth the $5 million it cost you to build it earlier in the year. By the way, the 10 pizza parlors are not worth the $2 million that it cost to build them either. So, if the factory and parlors are not worth what you paid for them, they are impaired. But the hard question is how much are they worth? How much of their cost do you need to write off in order to ensure they are valued correctly? There is, as in most cases, a somewhat logical answer. However, from an appropriate or **"fairly stated"** accounting position, there are sometimes several correct accounting methods based on **"generally accepted accounting principles" (GAAP)**. These principles tend to be rules-based and difficult to interpret. The answer is too complex for our current discussion. However, the idea was not to teach you how to perform appropriate valuations. Instead, it was to impress upon you the complexities involved and the importance of making appropriate valuation decisions.

Classification

Transactions are properly classified. Appropriate classification is another primarily accounting objective of management. It is as simple as classifying revenues as revenues and expenses as expenses. The mistakes are as simple as making accounting entry errors by using the wrong account. The errors can, however, be very significant as when a major telephone holding company misclassifies billions of dollars of current period expenses as capital. This incorrectly deferred the recognition of the expense to future periods and therefore incorrectly achieved millions of dollars in profits when the correct accounting classification would have produced millions of dollars in losses.

Timeliness/Cutoff

Transactions are recorded in the correct period — another appropriate accounting objective based on the accounting principle of periodicity. The periodicity principle says that a company's life can be split into multiple reporting periods and that you can correctly allocate or attribute revenues and expenses to each period in order to determine the profitability of the company for each period.

Important to this concept is that you are able to ensure that all of the accounting transactions are correctly and timely recorded into each period as you reach the end of a period and the beginning of the next. For example, the month ends for our pizza parlor on Sunday. Obviously, all sales for Sunday should be recorded in the current period and all sales on the following Monday should be recorded into the next period. However, what about the payroll that will be paid on the following Friday? The payroll will be for the last two weeks of the month ending on the Sunday. Obviously, the payroll is going to be paid for work that was performed during the current month, but the payment will not be made until after the current month has ended and the next begun.

One way to account for the payroll would be to record the expense only when paid. This is generally called the **"cash basis"** of accounting. However, cash basis accounting does not match the revenues earned with the expenses that were incurred to earn the revenues. In our case, recording the payroll expense on Friday as a current period expense would not match payroll expense with the revenues earned in the last two weeks of the prior month. So, in accounting, there is another principle — the matching principle. This principle says that revenues should be matched against the expenses that were incurred to earn the revenue. In order to achieve this, the payroll would be accrued or recorded in the current period rather than in the next. Companies that accrue revenues and expenses are using the **"accrual basis"** of accounting. As you can see, the issues related to the cutoff objective revolve around the recording of revenues and expenses in the right periods. If you intend to achieve this objective, you have to develop appropriate cutoff procedures.

Segregation of Duties

Appropriate segregation between the authorization of transactions, the recording of transactions and the maintenance of assets. The separation of these responsibilities is an important objective of management. The separation of these responsibilities protects not only the company, but also the employee. Fraud usually takes place because three conditions exist:

- Motive, which is usually tied to a financial need.
- Opportunity or weakness in the internal control structure that can be abused.
- Rationalization that allows the employee to somehow justify the fraud.

The above is termed the "Fraud Triangle" and is adapted from the training course "How Fraud Hurts You and Your Organization" sponsored by the American Institute of Certified Public Accountants (AICPA) and the Association of Certified Fraud Examiners (ACFE).

In many small companies, it may be impossible to appropriately separate these duties between several employees simply because the company does not have enough employees. When this is true, it is important that the manager responsible for this area review the work that is performed to ensure that employees do not avail themselves of the opportunities that exist due to the lack of adequate separation.

The review of the first-line manager is critical to the adequate prevention of fraud. Many frauds actually take place when an apparent adequate separation of duties is present, but one of the parties responsible for ensuring that this separation occurs is not performing his or her duties correctly. This individual is usually the first-line manager.

As an example, a friend of mine told me a story about an actual employee fraud that he found early in his career. He was a first-line accounting department manager and one of his responsibilities was to review the department's actual performance against the financial plan or budget. He had just taken over a new accounting department within his company, and he noticed after a couple of months that the payroll expense for one of his employees seemed to be changing every month. He thought this was curious and asked the employee about it. The employee said that there was nothing wrong. Now, as it turned out, one of the department manager's friends was the payroll department manager, so he called him up. The accounting department manager then pulled the time sheets, which he had reviewed and signed for his department, from their file. He selected a recent period and told the payroll manager how many hours were on this employee's time sheet. The payroll manager looked up the number of hours that they paid the employee, and the number of hours paid was greater than the number of hours on the accounting department's copy of the time sheet. The two managers compared a couple of more pay periods and each time the number of hours paid was actually more than what was recorded on the accounting department manager's time sheet. The payroll manager then pulled his copy of the time sheets that his department had received. The hours on these time sheets were actually greater than the hours recorded on the accounting department manager's original signed copies.

In this situation, there had been an appropriate segregation of duties established. There was a separate payroll department that only accepted and made changes to an employee's pay if these changes were appropriately authorized by management. This payroll department only paid employees if they received an appropriately completed and authorized time sheet from management (authorization of transactions). The payroll department generated everyone's paychecks and maintained the payroll records (recording of transactions). A different department maintained the cash accounts from which the paychecks were paid (maintenance of assets). There was an appropriate segregation of duties. An appropriate segregation of duties is assumed to exist if these three responsibilities are separated such that no single employee has more than one of them. So, what was the weakness? Was it that this employee discovered that she could change the hours on her own time sheet, since she forwarded all time sheets for the department to the payroll department, and that only she would know? Unfortunately, yes, this was the weakness in the actual internal controls in place that this employee used to increase her own paycheck. She did it simply by increasing the hours she reported to the payroll department.

To continue the story, this employee had worked in this department for many years, and she had worked for several different first-line managers during her tenure. The control weakness was that none of these managers had ever reviewed the payroll records closely enough, if at all, until my friend took over these responsibilities. Management has an inherent review responsibility to ensure that the established segregation of duties actually is operating as designed. In this specific case, a comparison of the time sheets to the payroll expense was necessary to ensure that incompatible duties and responsibilities were separated in such a way that a single employee was not able to commit and conceal errors, irregularities, and fraud. By this example, you should be able to see how important it is to not only ensure that your business processes are designed with an appropriate segregation of duties, but also how important it is to review your established segregations to ensure that they are operating as designed.

Safeguarding Assets

Assets are secured from theft, damage, and unauthorized access or usage. How would you feel if your cash was left out where people could just help themselves? Obviously, due to its liquidity or easy spend ability, most companies have pretty good access controls over cash. However, some of your most important assets are information, and many times this information is created and maintained within automated computer systems. These systems generally have automated security systems as part of the overall design. The primary objectives of these security systems are to safeguard assets, ensure an adequate segregation of duties, and accountability for actions.

To safeguard your information assets, first you want to ensure that only authorized personnel are allowed access and that the type of access granted is appropriate. Second, should something go wrong, you want to know who did what so that there is appropriate accountability for actions. Obviously, you would much rather prevent bad things from happening than have to correct them. This we will discuss later in much greater detail.

Sometimes inappropriate access is granted to employees, which creates an inappropriate risk. For example, one of your most valuable secrets could be the recipe for your pizza crust because your crusts are what set you apart from your competition. What if the recipe is kept on an automated system within a recipe program that had an automated access security program in which adequate access controls were implemented. However, the recipe database is readily readable if you were to open it directly outside of the program, and over 20 computer programmers have access to read and write to this database directly. Any one of these programmers could easily copy the database to a floppy disk and sell it to your competitors. Obviously over 20 programmers with this access is excessive. In fact, probably none of these programmers needs this access considering the exposure it creates. Wouldn't it be acceptable for them to only have this access on an emergency basis? From this example, we see some of the more complex situations and exposures that exist in attempting to ensure assets are appropriately safeguarded.

Control Objectives and Control Activities

The above objectives of management are called **"control objectives"** because, in its desire to control the activities of its employees, management has specific defined objectives (i.e., control objectives) that need to be achieved to ensure that these activities are appropriately controlled.

Appropriately controlled in this case, as in all cases, meaning that the specific control objectives for a process are achieved.

To enable the achievement of control objectives, management designs controls. So what is a control? Simply an activity used to enable the achievement of one or more control objectives, which is why they are usually called **"control activities."** Again, a control activity can be anything management has designed and implemented to ensure the achievement of a control objective. For example, to ensure the completeness control objective was achieved, someone invented and sold the cash register to management. By requiring employees to use the cash register to enter all sales transactions, management is attempting to ensure that all valid sales transactions are actually recorded. Our friend at the airport booth found a way around this control activity. Unfortunately, there are very few control activities that are able to guarantee the achievement of a control objective, which is why multiple control activities are usually used. A control activity that is used to ensure a control objective is achieved when the primary control activity (recording sales into the cash register) fails is called a mitigating control activity or **"mitigating control."** Mitigating controls attempt to limit the risk of bad things happening when the primary control activities fail to work properly. This brings us to the next question — how many and which control activities are needed?

The Adequacy of Control

If no single control activity can generally guarantee the achievement of a control objective, how many controls does it take, and do we really ever want to guarantee the achievement of a control objective? An important thing to remember is that the design and implementation of any control costs money. Therefore, there is a cost versus benefit trade-off involved in designing control activities. It is also important to understand that the control objectives do not change for a particular business process. This is because the control objectives are based on the inherent risks within the process. The inherent risks only change if the business process changes. The bad things that can go wrong are always there and waiting to go wrong if appropriate controls are not put in place. However, there are many different ways to achieve a given control objective. The exact controls, although consistent in some very limited cases, are usually specific to the exact circumstances of the business process.

Management is constantly struggling with the issue of how to obtain an adequacy of control at minimum cost. This struggle is not related to just one control or another but which combination of controls is best. Therefore, a control activity is not usually considered on its own but rather as part of a system of controls, and the achievement of a control objective is not usually determined based on a single control activity but rather on the system of controls established by management to achieve the control objective. When one attempts to determine the adequacy of control, one must review the system of controls that exists to achieve the control objectives. However, simply ensuring that a system of controls is in place that will achieve the control objectives is not enough to be able to determine if the level of control is adequate.

As mentioned earlier, businesses exist to make money and systems of control cost money. As with any other business expense, management must strive to achieve the maximum level of control that is reasonable based on the relative expense and risks. In other words, management can achieve its control objectives via the system of controls it has designed and implemented but at too high a cost. For example, if you want to have a bank vault that is absolutely safe you will probably need to have it underground in a deep cavern with multiple layers of embedded soldiers and tanks on each level. Why? Because to be absolutely safe you have to ensure that all risks are mitigated. Maybe you don't need this level of security to protect against your normal bank robbers. However, in the world today you should be concerned about foreign powers — right? Can the bank vault be protected against a foreign nuclear attack? I think so, but that is why we need the underground cavern with multiple layers of embedded soldiers and tanks on each level. Of course, your vault may cost $80 million to $90 million. What? Too expensive? Well, I agree. In fact, I am quite sure that any bank manager that would actually suggest such a vault would be considered crazy and told that he needed to work somewhere else. The point is that in evaluating the adequacy of control, management must consider the probable risks that must be faced and mitigated.

As management you may even decide to accept more risk in order to lower the cost of control. Is this a good decision? It depends. The determination of the risk of a failure of the system of control is a judgment call. The system of control usually does not fail if it is appropriately designed. If it fails, then and only then do we know the risk of failure. Usually we have to guess at what the risks are and the chance of the system of control failing based on our experience, judgment, and understanding of what is reasonable. To determine the right system of control for a given situation, management must rely upon their experience to determine a reasonable estimate of the risks and weigh this against the cost of implementing specific controls to mitigate these risks.

For another example, earlier I mentioned that the airport parking authority had a weakness in control because the attendants in the booths could defraud the company by not recording the transactions and pocketing the cash. Now, if you believe that the airport parking authority is aware of this risk, why would they allow such employee fraud to exist? In reality it may be based upon a conscious business analysis of the probable risk of fraud losses, with an appropriately calculated point estimate of these losses versus the cost of implementing tighter control processes (at least this is what one would hope). As always in business, the benefit of enhanced controls must outweigh the cost. At the time, the cost of improving the airport parking authority's controls may have been too great based on the estimated benefit — that improved control would have been achieved. However, as I said earlier, the search for an adequate system of control and an optimum balance between the cost and benefit of such a system is a never-ending struggle because things are constantly changing.

One of these changes has been the improvement of automated systems based on better computer and software technologies. In fact, a couple of years later when I was leaving that same airport, I learned that they had implemented a new set of control processes — made possible by a new automated system. With this new system, upon entry into the airport, the operators enter your license plate number into their new automated system, which automatically spits out an electronic receipt. The receipt is blank, except for an electronically encoded strip. The automated system used by the parking authority automatically records your arrival time on this strip when the operator enters your license plate number. When you leave the airport, you drive up to the booth and hand the operator the electronic receipt. He or she must swipe the receipt to determine how long you have been in the parking area. To do this, he or she must use the cash register to be able to read the encoded strip. Thus, there is an improvement in control because the only way to know how much to charge is to swipe the receipt, which automatically enters the amount owed into the cash register. Then, the cashier must either collect payment or call a supervisor to open the gate and let you out. In the old system, the flaw was that the entry and exit times were written on the parking receipt automatically by the parking gates and the parking booth attendant manually read the times, manually calculated the amount owned, and then, most of the time, entered the amount owed into the cash register. The weakness in control was that he or she could ask for the amount owed without entering it into the cash register for customers who were willing to forego a receipt. Due to this weakness in the control activities used by the parking authority, operators were able to steal from their employer.

So why didn't the parking authority implement this new automated system sooner? I am sure that it was cost prohibitive, and they may have had some mitigating controls upon which they were relying. For example, an attendant that got too greedy would take in a total amount of parking receipts that was out of line with the receipts taken in by the other attendants during the same time period. Over time, a trend would appear and management would be able to identify the attendants who were cheating the company. There may have been other mitigating controls, but they probably were not that good; after all, the parking authority did spend a lot of money implementing the new automated system. They must have believed that the savings based on a decreased risk of losses due to fraud would outweigh the cost of the new automated system by a sufficient amount to make this investment in enhanced controls profitable.

The Internal Audit Function

Now that we understand the difficulties involved in designing good systems of control, we can see why this is an ongoing, primary concern of management. In fact, almost everyone agrees that management should spend much of their time reviewing and developing controls. However, management would probably say that they are too busy trying to get their normal work done, along with all of those special projects that keep occurring, to have time to focus on controls as much as they should. This is the reason most companies need an internal audit function. If management had the time to review and update their control processes on a truly ongoing basis and actually had the training and expertise to accomplish this, then there would be no need for an internal audit function. However, in most medium to larger companies, there is a need for internal control specialized knowledge, ability, and availability.

Internal auditors have a very special and important purpose. They are an independent review process over the system of internal control that management implements, with the intent of ensuring the overall adequacy of this system. The manner in which this is supposed to occur is that the internal audit function performs a survey of all the auditable entities and areas within the company. Then, they use a risk-based approach to determine the relative risk of each area to each other area, and to the entity as a whole. Next, they determine — based on the overall level of acceptable risk — how often each area of the company should be reviewed. The audit universe, as this is termed, is then used to determine the areas within the company to audit each year. Based on inherent risk some areas are reviewed yearly (i.e., expense reports). Other areas may only need to be reviewed every fifth year.

The review that internal audit performs of all these areas is a review of the adequacy of the system of internal controls. Internal auditors generally use a review methodology where they determine management's control objectives for an area being reviewed. They then obtain an understanding of the specifics of the business process so that they can determine the controls in place. They then map these controls against management's control objectives to determine control design adequacy — if the control objectives are achieved or if there are missing controls. Next, they will test the controls that were determined to be in place and determine if they are operating as designed. For controls that are missing or are not operating as designed, they will make recommendations for improvement. So, the purpose of the internal audit function is to assist management in the review of the system of controls. And, although internal auditors work with all levels of the company's management, they cannot be part of this management team because they need to be independent of management to be able to be effective in evaluating the system of internal control. Therefore, although they work with all of the management team, internal audit as a function should generally report to the audit committee.

The Audit Committee

The audit committee is required to be composed of at least three outside members of the board of directors. The audit committee members must all have appropriate financial expertise, and at least one member must meet the qualifications necessary to be considered a **"financial expert."** The audit committee has several functions. However, one of its primary objectives is to review the work of the internal auditors, external auditors, and management and to ensure that the overall system of internal controls is adequate. Equally important, the audit committee is interested in ensuring that this system of internal control is adequate to ensure that the financial and other information produced by the company meets a standard of overall material accuracy and fair presentation.

When you take the system of control that management implements and you add to it the internal audit function and the audit committee, you have what is generally called the system of internal control. All of this is used as a single process to control the company's internal business processes and to ensure an adequate level of control based on reasonable cost benefit trade-offs and assumptions of acceptable financial risk.

Chapter Summary

This discussion of internal control is actually somewhat theoretical in that it was intended to give readers — who are not internal controls experts — a background that is sufficient upon which to build an understanding of key controls. Actual internal control experts might even object to some of the simplicity with which I have described what are in fact very complex processes. However, my intent is to be truthful to the theoretical basis of internal control and provide you with the basis you will need to understand the rest of this book. To test this theory, below is the COSO definition of internal control. With the background I provided above, this definition should be informative to you now. One last point: the Securities and Exchange Commission (SEC) has mandated that all publicly traded companies adopt an authoritative internal control framework, and since COSO's framework is the one most companies are going to adopt, COSO's definition is probably the definition of internal control for most SEC registrants.

COSO'S Definition of Internal Control

Copyright © 1991 by the American Institute of Certified Public Accountants, Inc. Reprinted with permission.

Internal control is a process, affected by an entity's board of directors, management, and other personnel, designed to provide reasonable assurance regarding the achievement of objectives in the following categories:

- Effectiveness and efficiency of operations
- Reliability of financial reporting
- Compliance with applicable laws and regulations

Key Concepts

- Internal control is a *process*. It is a means to an end, not an end in itself.
- Internal control is effected by *people*. It is not merely policy manuals and forms, but people at every level of an organization.
- Internal control can be expected to provide only *reasonable assurance*, not absolute assurance, to an entity's management and board.
- Internal control is geared to the achievement of *objectives* in one or more separate but overlapping categories.

CHAPTER 2
WHY YOU NEED A
KEY CONTROLS PROCESS

> "The scandal, which it causes, constitutes the offence,
> and sinning in secret is no sinning at all."
> — Tartuffe the Imposter

I wish I could convince you that the best reason to develop a key controls process for your company is because it is a good management practice. A key controls process is an ongoing, self-audit quality control and assurance process that enables management to ensure that their financial and other significant process objectives are accomplished in a complete, accurate, and timely manner. However, if it were as easy to convince you of this as it is to say, then you would probably already have a key controls process. Assuming you do not, then there are other reasons why you are probably interested in developing an ongoing internal control evaluation and reporting process. Of course, these reasons are probably to ensure compliance with the requirements of the Sarbanes-Oxley Act of 2002. This chapter is designed to help you understand what these new requirements are in relation to the review and certification of a company's internal control processes, and for those companies that must comply, what the potential risks are of noncompliance. In later chapters, we will explain what a key controls process is and why I believe it is the best solution for Sarbanes-Oxley Act compliance, although I plan to give a lot of hints at the end of this chapter. Right now, let's start with the pre-Sarbanes-Oxley Act requirements.

After the stock market crash of 1929 and during the era of American history called the Great Depression, Congress passed the Securities Act of 1933 and the Securities Exchange Act of 1934 to restore investor confidence in our capital markets. These laws had two primary purposes. First, to regulate the activities of the people and companies who sell securities to the public in order to ensure that the public is treated fairly, and second to ensure that companies who publicly offer their securities tell the truth about their businesses. In addition, the Securities and Exchange Commission (SEC) was created to ensure compliance with these new laws.

As part of the reforms coming out of this era, companies that raised capital by selling either debt or equity instruments to the public were required to register with the SEC. These "registrants" were also required to file many different reports with the commission that became public and were intended to ensure these companies materially disclosed the truth about their businesses, the securities they sold, and the risks involved in investing in the company. Another measure to ensure the fair presentation of the financial information disclosed in these reports was taken — the imposition of a requirement that these public companies have an independent audit performed of their books and records. The intent of this independent audit is to examine the company's financial statements in order to express an opinion on the fairness with which these statements and the assertions embodied within them **present fairly in all material respects** the financial position, results of operations, and changes in financial position of the registrant for the periods reviewed in conformity with generally accepted accounting principles (i.e., all of the accounting rules). Further, the audit must be performed in conformity with all of the auditing standards in effect at the time of the audit (i.e., all of the auditing rules, required review procedures, and quality standards).

The registrant's financial statements are only a small part of the total required financial information and analysis that management is required to disclose in the reports the SEC requires management to file. As stated on the SEC's Web site:

> The Commission requires public companies to disclose meaningful financial and other information to the public, which provides a common pool of knowledge for all investors to use to judge for themselves if a company's securities are a good investment. Only through the steady flow of timely, comprehensive, and accurate information can people make sound investment decisions.

The Sarbanes-Oxley Act of 2002

The Sarbanes-Oxley Act has enabled the SEC to enhance the requirements that ensure full and meaningful disclosure so that they can better achieve this objective. The *Public Company Accounting Reform and Investor Protection Act of 2002*, commonly known as the Sarbanes-Oxley Act, which was signed into law by President Bush on July 30, 2002, is the most comprehensive and extensive set of enhancements to the exchange acts since the original laws passed in 1933 and 1934 and had the same objective as the original acts — to restore investor confidence. This irony and everything that led to it is a subject for another book. In this chapter, we are going to concern ourselves with the impact of only three sections of the Sarbanes-Oxley Act:

- SEC 302 Corporate Responsibility for Financial Reports
- SEC 404 Management Assessment of Internal Controls
- SEC 906 Corporate Responsibility for Financial Reports

Section 302 requires the company's senior management to certify that they are responsible for ensuring that the company has adequate internal controls to ensure full disclosure of all of the registrant's material information and the fair and reliable presentation in all material respects of the company's financial statements. That the company's senior management has evaluated the company's **disclosure controls and procedures** for the period and disclosed their conclusions about the effectiveness of such controls. That they have disclosed in the report material changes in **internal control over financial reporting**. And, that they have disclosed to the audit committee and their independent auditor all **significant deficiencies** and **material weaknesses** in the design and operation of internal control over financial reporting. Finally, that they have disclosed any fraud involving management with a significant role in the registrant's internal control over financial reporting.

All of the terms in bold type above will be explained later in this chapter. Let's begin with the first one.

Present Fairly in All Material Respects

The SEC has stated that the Sarbanes-Oxley Act Section 302 certifications are not to be limited to a representation that the financial statements have been presented in accordance with generally accepted accounting principles (GAAP). Instead, the SEC stated that:

> The certification statement regarding fair presentation of financial statements and other financial information is not limited to a representation that the financial statements and other financial information have been presented in accordance with "generally accepted accounting principles" and is not otherwise limited by reference to generally accepted accounting principles. We believe that Congress intended this statement to provide assurances that the financial information disclosed in a report, viewed in its entirety, meets a standard of overall material accuracy and completeness that is broader than financial reporting requirements under generally accepted accounting principles. In our view, a "fair presentation" of an issuer's financial condition, results of operations, and cash flows encompasses the selection of appropriate accounting policies, proper application of appropriate accounting policies, disclosure of financial information that is informative and reasonably reflects the underlying transactions and events, and the inclusion of any additional disclosure necessary to provide investors with a materially accurate and complete picture of an issuer's financial condition, results of operations, and cash flows.

Materiality

In financial reporting, the risk that must be mitigated is that material information would not be adequately or correctly disclosed to the people who rely upon this information in making decisions related to the company's public debt and equity securities. Therefore, the question becomes what is material? The determination of materiality is judgmental, based upon both quantitative and qualitative criteria. However, information should be considered material if its inclusion, omission, or misstatement, in light of surrounding circumstances, makes it probable that the judgment of a reasonable person relying on the information would be changed or influenced by the omission or misstatement. There is no numerical threshold in the determination of materiality. So, if you are familiar with it, please forget the five percent rule. All of the pertinent circumstances around an issue or issues should be considered before determining materiality and inclusion or exclusion from an SEC report. For financial omissions, the effect of the items should be considered both singularly and in total. This is a somewhat simplistic rule for materiality; however, it will work well for a general understanding. For a detailed understanding, one should consult the SEC's *Staff Accounting Bulletin No. 99*. We will discuss materiality again in Chapters 6 and 11.

Sarbanes-Oxley Section 906

Section 906 requires company senior management to certify, at the risk of imprisonment, for false statements that the company's financial statements fairly present in all material respects the company's financial position and results of operations. Second, that the company has fully complied with all Securities Exchange Act of 1934 requirements. Unlike Sarbanes-Oxley Section 302 above and Section 404 below, which amend the Exchange Act's, Section 906 is a criminal provision and amends the federal criminal code. The required certification must be made and filed with all periodic reports by the registrant's chief executive and chief financial officers. The Justice Department will administer any criminal penalties for failure to comply with the requirements of Section 906, which include a fine of up to $1 million and imprisonment for up to 10 years or both for knowingly making and filing a false certification. A willful violation can be punished by a fine of up to $5 million and imprisonment for up to 20 years or both.

Sarbanes-Oxley Act Section 404

In Section 404 of the Sarbanes-Oxley Act, Congress enacted a law that requires each annual report that a company (public registrant), other than a registered investment company, files pursuant to the Exchange Act to contain an internal control report: (1) stating management's responsibilities for establishing and maintaining adequate internal control structure and procedures for financial reporting; and (2) containing an assessment, as of the end of the company's most recent fiscal year, of the effectiveness of the company's internal controls and procedures for financial reporting.

It is Section 404 of the Sarbanes-Oxley Act that is having and will have the most significant effect on companies because it requires management to develop an internal control review process that must support an annual independent audit. However, one needs to understand that the ongoing internal control review process developed must also enable quarterly compliance with the Section 302 requirements. Although the level of review required under Section 302 is not as in-depth as that required under Section 404 (as will be explained more later), the set of internal controls that must be reviewed is broader under Section 302. Therefore, the internal control review process that management must design and implement must enable an evaluation on a quarterly basis of both management's disclosure controls and procedures and internal control over financial reporting. The controls to be reviewed do not change from quarter to quarter. What changes is how the controls need to be reviewed in order to support the quarterly Section 302 Certification and the annual Section 404 management report.

In addition, if a company is going to build a system of ongoing internal control review to satisfy both Section 404 and 302 requirements, does it not make sense to gain the most benefit from this investment? To do such, why not develop an ongoing self-audit quality control and assurance process that enables management to ensure that their financial and other significant process objectives are accomplished in a complete, accurate, and timely manner on a monthly, quarterly, and annual basis while ensuring compliance with Sarbanes-Oxley Act requirements? This is what a key controls process will do.

The SEC, pursuant to the requirements of the actual act, developed and adopted final rules under Section 404 of the Sarbanes-Oxley Act. Per the final rules as promulgated by the SEC:

> The final rules require a company's annual report to include an internal control report of management that contains:
>
> - A statement of management's responsibility for establishing and maintaining adequate internal control over financial reporting for the company;
> - A statement identifying the framework used by management to conduct the required evaluation of the effectiveness of the company's internal control over financial reporting;
> - Management's assessment of the effectiveness of the company's internal control over financial reporting as of the end of the company's most recent fiscal year, including a statement as to whether or not the company's internal control over financial reporting is effective. The assessment must include disclosure of any "material weaknesses" in the company's internal control over financial reporting identified by management. Management is not permitted to conclude that the company's internal control over financial reporting is effective if there are one or more material weaknesses in the company's internal control over financial reporting; and
> - A statement that the registered public accounting firm that audited the financial statements included in the annual report has issued an attestation report on management's assessment of the registrant's internal control over financial reporting.
>
> As proposed, our final rules also require a company to file, as part of the company's annual report, the attestation report of the registered public accounting firm that audited the company's financial statements.

The final rules do not specify the exact content of the proposed management report, as the SEC stated in its proposed rules. It believes that this would likely result in boilerplate responses of little value. The SEC stated that they believe that management should tailor the report to the company's specific circumstances.

Public companies with public float exceeding $75 million will be required to comply with these requirements as of the end of their first fiscal year ending on or after June 15, 2004. Smaller companies, foreign private issuers, and companies with only debt securities will have until fiscal years ending on or after April 15, 2004, to comply.

Section 404 above, requires that the company provide a statement identifying the framework used by management to evaluate the effectiveness of the company's internal control over financial reporting. In Chapter 9 we will discuss the available frameworks and why most companies will adopt the Committee of Sponsoring Organizations of the Treadway Commission (COSO) framework. We will also explain how to apply the COSO framework.

Internal Control Over Financial Reporting

The Commission's final Sarbanes-Oxley Act Section 404 rules defined a new set or population of internal controls with which the reader must be familiar in order to comply with the rules. The Commission's final rules define "internal control over financial reporting" as:

> A process designed by, or under the supervision of, the registrant's principal executive and principal financial officers, or persons performing similar functions, and effected by the registrant's board of directors, management, and other personnel, to provide reasonable assurance regarding the reliability of financial reporting and the preparation of financial statements for external purposes in accordance with generally accepted accounting principles and includes those policies and procedures that:
>
> (1) Pertain to the maintenance of records that in reasonable detail accurately and fairly reflect the transactions and dispositions of the assets of the registrant;
> (2) Provide reasonable assurance that transactions are recorded as necessary to permit preparation of financial statements in accordance with generally accepted accounting principles, and that receipts and expenditures of the registrant are being made only in accordance with authorizations of management and directors of the registrant; and
> (3) Provide reasonable assurance regarding prevention or timely detection of unauthorized acquisition, use, or disposition of the registrant's assets that could have a material effect on the financial statements.

We recognize that our definition of the term "internal control over financial reporting" reflected in the final rules encompasses the subset of internal controls addressed in the COSO Report that pertains to financial reporting objectives. Our definition does not encompass the elements of the COSO Report definition that relate to effectiveness and efficiency of a company's operations and a company's compliance with applicable laws and regulations, with the exception of compliance with the applicable laws and regulations directly related to the preparation of financial statements, such as the Commission's financial reporting requirements. Our definition is consistent with the description of internal accounting controls in Exchange Act Section 13(b)(2)(B).

Internal Control Over Financial Reporting Versus Disclosure Controls and Procedures

There is another class of controls that management is already required to review on a quarterly basis. Sarbanes-Oxley Act Section 302 rules require a company's certifying officers, which is generally the chief executive and chief financial officers, to certify on a quarterly basis that they are responsible for establishing and maintaining disclosure controls and procedures and have:

- Designed such disclosure controls and procedures to ensure that material registrant information is made know to them.
- Evaluated the effectiveness of the registrant's disclosure controls and procedures and presented their conclusions about the effectiveness of such as of the end of the period covered by this report.

(Please see Chapter 11 for a detailed discussion of the Section 302 Certification requirements.)

Disclosure Controls and Procedures

So what are disclosure controls and procedures? This is another new term the SEC developed. Disclosure controls and procedures are a set of internal controls that includes most of the internal control over financial reporting, although potentially not all, which we will discuss more in the next section. Disclosure controls and procedures include:

Controls and procedures of a company that are designed to ensure that information required to be disclosed by the company in the reports that it files or submits under the Exchange Act is recorded, processed, summarized, and reported within the time periods specified in the Commission's rules and forms. The definition further states that disclosure controls and procedures include, without limitation, controls and procedures designed to ensure that the information required to be disclosed by a company in the reports that it files or submits under the Exchange Act is accumulated and communicated to the company's management, including its principal executive and principal financial officers, or persons performing similar functions, as appropriate to allow timely decisions regarding required disclosure.

The SEC interpreted disclosure controls and procedures to include most internal controls and procedures for financial reporting as well as controls designed to ensure compliance with the Commission's disclosure requirements beyond the financial statements (e.g., management's discussion and analysis, executive compensation, legal proceedings). The SEC's intent was to develop a broader concept that includes not only the traditional internal control over financial reporting, but also controls over the disclosure of all material financial and nonfinancial information in Exchange Act reports.

Difference Between Disclosure Controls and Procedures and Internal Control Over Financial Reporting

A company's disclosure controls and procedures, as per the SEC, "will include those components of internal control over financial reporting that provide reasonable assurances that transactions are recorded as necessary to permit preparation of financial statements in accordance with generally accepted accounting principles."

Although there will be considerable overlap between a company's disclosure controls and procedures and its internal control over financial reporting, the SEC stated that it believes that there will be both disclosure controls and procedures that are not part of the company's internal control over financial reporting, and that there will be controls that are part of internal control over financial reporting that are not part of the company's disclosure controls and procedures. It will be very important to ensure that all of the company's internal controls that are disclosure controls and procedures are specifically identified and evaluated each quarter. This will include all disclosure controls and procedures that are part of internal control over financial reporting. Therefore, since there is considerable overlap between these two sets of controls, the assumption that a company will not have to evaluate most of its internal control over financial reporting on an ongoing quarterly basis is incorrect. The SEC explained, however, that the quarterly evaluation of disclosure controls and procedures should be based on an evaluation of the overall effectiveness of the disclosure controls and procedures. That a company's management has the ability to focus such evaluation on changes since the most recent evaluation, such as areas of specific weakness, continuing areas of concern, or other significant aspects of the company's disclosure controls and procedures that merit review.

In a footnote to the final rules, the SEC explained that management could make a correct determination that a lesser level of review procedures is necessary to review an internal control over financial reporting that is "subsumed" within the disclosure controls and procedures during a quarterly evaluation than would be needed for the annual review and attestation.

From this guidance, it appears that the procedures necessary to support an evaluation of the internal control over financial reporting component of disclosure controls and procedures on a quarterly basis are less than what is necessary for the annual review and should be focused on changes since the last annual review. However, management should perform its review of the design and operation of the company's internal control over financial reporting for the required annual evaluation over a period of time adequate to ensure, as of the end of the company's fiscal year, that the design and operation are effective. In addition, an overall conclusion as to the adequacy of the company's disclosure controls and procedures is required quarterly. Therefore, the population of controls that must be reviewed and opined upon does not change from quarter to quarter. What changes are the review procedures necessary to ensure adequate support exists for the assertions that management is required to make. I suggest working closely with the company's external auditor to ensure adequate coverage is achieved for both the quarterly and annual evaluations. Also, one should note that testing of internal control over financial reporting to ensure these controls are effective could take place year round.

The key control processes explained later in this book are intended to enable you to achieve compliance for both these annual and quarterly Sarbanes-Oxley evaluation, certification, and reporting requirements. The key controls processes are intended to enable this compliance in the most cost effective and efficient manner. One of the fundamental concepts of the key controls process is the establishment of a **frequency of review** for key controls. Review frequencies are normally monthly, quarterly, and yearly. Key controls are identified and then reviewed based on these frequencies — both to provide assurance to management that the right things are being done right and to enable compliance with the annual and quarterly Sarbanes-Oxley evaluation, certification, and reporting requirements. **Minimum standards of control** are developed to ensure an adequate quality of control is achieved for each key control and to ensure again adequate support for compliance with the annual and quarterly Sarbanes-Oxley evaluation, certification, and reporting requirements. Due to the significant events and judgments risk assessment and reporting process component of a key controls process, management can not only focus and ensure adequate mitigation of key control issues, but can ensure adequate risk management of potential and actual business process risks.

Quarterly Disclosure of Material Changes in Internal Control Over Financial Reporting

The SEC also made changes to the Sarbanes-Oxley Section 302 quarterly certification requirements in their final Section 404 rules release:

> Under our final rules, a company also will be required to evaluate and disclose any change in its internal control over financial reporting that occurred during the fiscal quarter that has materially affected, or is reasonably likely to materially affect, the company's internal control over financial reporting.

Currently, all companies must comply with the above requirement. However, the companies will be making this disclosure based only on internal control over financial reporting, which is subsumed within disclosure controls and procedures. A company must begin to comply with the above requirement in its first periodic report due after the first annual report required to include a management report on internal control over financial reporting for the entire population of controls that embody internal control over financial reporting. As one would assume, the differences between these two populations of controls is both small and difficult to define. Therefore, for all intensive purposes, this requirement is in effect currently, and a company must disclose any change in its internal control over financial reporting that occurred during the fiscal quarter that has materially affected or is reasonably likely to materially affect the company's internal control over financial reporting. Any change in a company's internal control over financial reporting that is to mitigate a material weakness, which will be defined and explained shortly, would meet this requirement and need to be disclosed in the quarter in which the controls were changed. Since materiality is based on qualitative rather than quantitative factors, nonfinancial material changes in internal control over financial reporting would also need to be disclosed.

Purpose of Sarbanes-Oxley Section 404

The purpose of Section 404 is to enable the financial markets to discount the quality of a company's internal control processes into its market valuation. There is an inherent assumption in this purpose that the financial markets will believe that companies with poor internal control should be valued less than companies with strong internal control. This is a brave new world. For in it a company can still have an unqualified financial audit opinion and face financial uncertainty depending on the outcome of its internal control audit and the internal control audit opinion the company receives.

Prior to Section 404, independent audit firms reviewed internal control only to determine the nature, extent, and timing of later substantive tests. The scope of this review was limited and the results of such a review were confidential and reported generally only to the company's audit committee and certain members of the company's management who had a need to know. Now, because of Section 404, independent audit firms will perform a detailed review of internal control over financial reporting with a specific goal to be able to attest to their concurrence with management's report and assertions. Any **material weaknesses**, as currently proposed by the Public Company Accounting Oversight Board (PCAOB) and required by the SEC, will be disclosed in a company's annual report and will be discounted in the financial markets.

In this brave new world:

- GIVEN that we do not know how the financial markets will react to Section 404 disclosure of material weaknesses.
- GIVEN that the financial markets have not generally reacted well to "bad news" and although the past is not a guaranteed predictor of the future — this trend is probably going to continue.
- GIVEN that per the SEC's final rules implementing Section 404 "management is not permitted to conclude that the registrant's internal control over financial reporting is effective if there are one or more material weaknesses in the registrant's internal control over financial reporting."
- GIVEN that the effect of finding a material weakness and having an adverse auditor's opinion upon the company is unknown.
- THEREFORE, company management should determine the types of processes that need to be developed in order to ensure that they can implement and maintain on an ongoing basis a system of internal control evaluation and risk mitigation that will enable compliance

with Sarbanes-Oxley Sections 404 and 302 annual and quarterly requirements in the most efficient and effective manner. And, the purpose of this book is to help management achieve this objective.

PCAOB Exposure Draft

The Public Company Accounting Oversight Board (PCAOB) was established by the Sarbanes-Oxley Act as a nongovernmental, nonprofit corporate entity to perform oversight of the public accounting profession. This includes the adoption of ethical and quality control standards for use in the preparation of audit reports. In compliance with this mission, the PCAOB has proposed an auditing standard titled, "An Audit of Internal Control Over Financial Reporting Performed in Conjunction With an Audit of Financial Statements." As the name infers, the PCAOB auditing standard, in compliance with Sarbanes-Oxley Act Section 404(b), requires an integrated audit of internal control and financial statements. The integrated audit will produce two audit opinions: one on internal control over financial reporting, and a second on the fair presentation of the company's financial statements. These rules are intended to give guidance to the auditing profession in relation to how Sarbanes-Oxley Act Section 404 reviews should be conducted.

PCAOB Proposed Auditing Standard Review Process

First, management must develop an assessment process that adequately explains, documents, and tests both the design and the operation of their internal control over financial reporting. This process must be adequate to prove the effectiveness of internal control over financial reporting. According to the PCAOB's proposed auditing standard:

> The proposed standard would provide the auditor with criteria to use in evaluating the adequacy of management's documentation. Inadequate documentation would be considered an internal control deficiency, the severity of which the auditor would evaluate just as he or she would be required to evaluate the severity of other internal control deficiencies.

> The proposed auditing standard would allow the auditor to use, to a reasonable degree, the work performed by others, including management. Thus, the more extensive and reliable management's assessment is, the less extensive and costly the auditor's work will need to be.

Second, management will propose an internal controls report to be included in their annual report for each SEC registrant. The independent auditor will audit management's internal control over financial reporting to determine their concurrence with management's assertions as made in management's report, and will issue a standard opinion for publication in the registrant's annual report. According to the PCAOB's proposed auditing standard:

The auditor's objective is to express an opinion about whether management's assessment, or conclusion, on the effectiveness of internal control over financial reporting is stated fairly in all material respects

The auditor needs to evaluate management's assessment process to be satisfied that management has an appropriate basis for its conclusion. The auditor, however, also needs to test the effectiveness of internal control to be satisfied that management's conclusion is correct and, therefore, fairly stated.

The proposed auditing standard would require that the auditor obtain evidence about the operating effectiveness of internal control over financial reporting for all relevant assertions for all significant accounts or disclosures.

Under the final Section 404 rules, in their annual reports, management must disclose material weaknesses. Per the SEC's final rules as already quoted above, a company's annual report must include an internal control report of management that contains:

Management's assessment of the effectiveness of the company's internal control over financial reporting as of the end of the company's most recent fiscal year, including a statement as to whether or not the company's internal control over financial reporting is effective. The assessment must include disclosure of any "material weaknesses" in the company's internal control over financial reporting identified by management. Management is not permitted to conclude that the company's internal control over financial reporting is effective if there are one or more material weaknesses in the company's internal control over financial reporting.

Since the SEC's final rules implementing Section 404 above state that management cannot conclude that the company's internal control over financial reporting is effective if there are one or more material weaknesses, the PCAOB has stated that management must conclude, if a material weakness is found, that internal control over financial reporting is ineffective in their management report and that the auditor must issue an adverse opinion. This audit opinion would also state that internal control over financial reporting is ineffective.

Internal Control Deficiencies

The determination of weaknesses in internal control and the severity of such is a judgmental issue. However, since this determination and judgment can have the most severe effect, it is important that we understand how these judgments are made. Weaknesses in internal control are called internal control deficiencies by the auditor. According to the PCAOB's auditing standard exposure draft:

An internal control deficiency exists when the design or operation of a control does not allow management or employees, in the normal course of performing their assigned functions, to prevent or detect misstatements on a timely basis.

- A deficiency in design exists when (a) a control necessary to meet the control objective is missing or (b) an existing control is not properly designed so that even if the control operates as designed, the control objective is not always met.
- A deficiency in operation exists when a properly designed control does not operate as designed, or when the person performing the control does not possess the necessary authority or qualifications to perform the control effectively.

A significant deficiency is an internal control deficiency that adversely affects the company's ability to initiate, record, process, or report external financial data reliably in accordance with generally accepted accounting principles. A significant deficiency could be a single deficiency, or a combination of deficiencies, that results in more than a remote likelihood that a misstatement of the annual or interim financial statements that is more than inconsequential in amount will not be prevented or detected.

A material weakness is a significant deficiency that, by itself, or in combination with other significant deficiencies, results in more than a remote likelihood that a material misstatement of the annual or interim financial statements will not be prevented or detected.

To summarize the above, a deficiency in internal control can result from an ineffective design of an internal control or from the ineffective operation of the internal control. An internal control **design deficiency** would exist if:

- A control activity was missing that was required to ensure the achievement of a control objective.
- A control objective was not achieved by a control activity or set of control activities.

An internal control **operating deficiency** would exist if:

- A control is determined to not be operating as designed, which is normally determined during testing of the control's operation.
- The person performing the control is determined to not have the authority or qualifications needed to perform the control correctly

Inadequate documentation of the design of internal control over financial reporting and/or the absence of sufficient documentation of the effective operation of internal control over financial reporting would in itself be considered an internal control deficiency, the severity of which would have to be evaluated by the auditor. The auditor could conclude that the inadequate documentation is a deficiency, a significant deficiency, or a material weakness. Additionally, inadequate documentation could result in a scope limitation, and the auditor cannot issue an unqualified opinion if there were any significant restrictions on the scope of the auditor's work. A significant scope limitation would require the auditor to express a qualified opinion or a disclaimer of opinion depending on the severity of the scope limitation.

Internal control deficiencies can range in severity from inconsequential to material, and a significant degree of judgment is required in determining the significance of deficiencies. In one's attempt to determine the severity of an internal control deficiency, and whether that deficiency could be significant or material, one should consider all of the relevant factors. Due to the complexity of such a decision process, no list can completely explain all of the potentially relevant factors in such a decision or their individual relevance. However, for example only, here are some of the factors that should be considered:

- The range of amounts of potential financial misstatement that could result from the deficiency and the probability that such a misstatement could be material and not be detected or prevented in a timely manner.
- The risk that a combination or repeated instances of deficiencies would result in a cumulative misstatement that may be material.
- The financial significance of the types and/or volume of transactions, account balances, and disclosures that are effected by the deficiency.
- The overall control environment and other mitigating controls that exist.

The existence of an internal control deficiency is based on the potential or probability that a financial statement misstatement exists. It is not necessary for there to have been an actual financial misstatement. Therefore, a material weakness in internal control can exist even though no actual material misstatement was found. For example, an inadequate financial reporting process or inadequate internal control documentation could both result in a material weakness, even though no actual material financial misstatement was found. According to the PCAOB's proposed auditing standard:

126. Each of the following circumstances should be regarded as at least a significant deficiency and is a strong indicator that a material weakness in internal control over financial reporting exists:

- Restatement of previously issued financial statements to reflect the correction of a misstatement.
- Identification by the auditor of a material misstatement in financial statements in the current period that was not initially identified by the company's internal control over financial reporting. (This is still a strong indicator of a material weakness even if management subsequently corrects the misstatement.)

- Oversight of the company's external financial reporting and internal control over financial reporting by the company's audit committee is ineffective. (Paragraphs 56 through 59 present factors to evaluate when determining whether the audit committee is ineffective.)
- For larger, more complex entities, the internal audit function or the risk assessment function is ineffective.
- For complex entities in highly regulated industries, an ineffective regulatory compliance function.
- Identification of fraud of any magnitude on the part of senior management.
- Significant deficiencies that have been communicated to management and the audit committee remain uncorrected after some reasonable period of time.

As stated above, if material misstatements are not detected timely by management and are found by the external auditor's procedures, then this is a strong indicator of a material weakness in the entity's internal controls. It will be management's task to justify sufficiently to the external auditor why such an occurrence should not be considered a material weakness. Obviously, this is a situation to be avoided. It should be noted that this is a considerable change over the current environment in which management would record an adjustment and the issue would essentially be resolved. Due to the need for enhanced control in this area, we will discuss this area in depth in Chapter 11.

Before we leave this discussion of the types of internal control deficiencies and what should be disclosed, I want to suggest that there is another type of internal control deficiency in addition to material weakness that needs to be identified and prevented, and if not prevented adequately, then disclosed. This is the "significant negative competitive practice." As this is an entirely new term and concept, Chapter 13 is devoted to this subject.

Consequences of Sarbanes-Oxley Act Noncompliance

Earlier, we discussed Sarbanes-Oxley Section 906 (which is an amendment to the federal criminal code) and the legal consequences of inadequate compliance. You might be wondering what the potential penalties are for failure to comply with these new requirements and the Exchange Act of 1934 in general. Sarbanes-Oxley Act Section 1106 increased the criminal penalties for securities act violations, and these penalties are now:

- An individual who engages in a willful violation of the Exchange Act of 1934 faces up to a $5 million fine (up from $1 million) and imprisonment for not more than 20 years (up from 10 years).
- The fine for entities that willfully violate the Exchange Act of 1934 was increased to $25 million from $2.5 million.

Sarbanes-Oxley Act Sections 302 and 404 are amendments to the Exchange Act of 1934; therefore, these penalties would apply to willful violation of these requirements by the principle executive and financial officers of SEC registrant companies. This, one would assume, will encourage registrant management to maintain adequate disclosure controls and procedures that include adequate internal control over financial reporting.

Key Controls Versus Self-assessments

It appears that some companies might attempt to enable their compliance with the Sarbanes-Oxley Act Section 404 and 302 internal control review requirements by developing self-assessments of their internal control processes. These self-assessments will, for the most part, be questionnaires of management with COSO-based internal control questions that management will answer for their areas of responsibility based only on their personal knowledge. I do not believe that the use of management self-assessments is an adequate approach to achieve compliance. Since the use of a self-assessment approach is probably the greatest potential contrast to a key controls process, we will compare these two approaches to assist you in understanding why a key controls approach is the best choice. Here are the top 10 reasons:

The 10th Best Reason Is:

A key controls process is an ongoing, monthly self-audit process where key internal controls are identified and reviewed/tested by comparing the actual results against established standards in order to give assurance to management that the right things are being done right. The self-evaluations are based solely on the knowledge of management, which is good, but how much knowledge do you need to make statements to the best of your knowledge?

The 9th Best Reason Is:

A key controls process will not only timely identify internal control deficiencies, but it will also enable management to manage the issues identified. The key controls process as explained later in this book requires the reporting of the deficiencies along with the appropriate mitigation of the deficiency. A self-evaluation questionnaire may help identify known issues; however, will it ensure that these identified internal control deficiencies are appropriately understood and mitigated?

The 8th Best Reason Is:

An integrated part of the key controls methodology, which will be explained in Chapter 7, is an ongoing, monthly, embedded risk self-assessment and reporting process. This process will enable management to not only identify control environment risks but to efficiently and effectively management them.

The 7th Best Reason Is:

The key controls process is an ongoing, monthly quality control and assurance process. A key controls process enables management to ensure and give assurance that process control objectives are being achieved so that business objectives can be achieved. Self-evaluation questionnaires are not.

The 6th Best Reason Is:

If management fails to find existing material weaknesses, then the company's external auditor will find them. Company management will be required by their external auditor to disclose the material weaknesses in their annual report and conclude that their internal control over financial reporting is ineffective in their Sarbanes-Oxley Section 404 required management internal control report. The external auditor will also issue an adverse opinion on internal control over financial reporting to be published in the company's annual report. This will subject the company to an unknown level of risk in the financial markets based on how these markets respond. Is a self-evaluation questionnaire approach going to enable you to identify and mitigate these deficiencies and the potential financial risks?

The 5th Best Reason Is:

Registrants are currently required to review their disclosure controls and procedures on a quarterly basis. Most of their internal controls over financial reporting are "subsumed," or a part of the company's disclosure controls and procedures. Companies are also currently required to review their internal control over financial reporting in order to be able to ensure appropriate mitigation and disclosure of material changes in such that occurred during the fiscal quarter that have materially affected, or are reasonably likely to materially affect, the company's internal control over financial reporting. How well will a questionnaire facilitate these requirements on an ongoing basis?

The 4th Best Reason Is:

External auditors will require public registrants to have adequate documentation of both the design and operation of their internal control over financial reporting so that they are able to perform their review. If you do not have adequate documentation, this in itself could be a reportable exception, which could result in an adverse audit opinion or a significant scope limitation and disclaimer of opinion. How well is the self-assessment questionnaire going to help you achieve this objective? How well is it going to assist with this objective over time?

The 3rd Best Reason Is:

The cost of an internal controls audit can be big. Two companies of equal size can pay as much as 100 percent to 200 percent more or less than the other company, depending on the quality of their internal control processes and the documentation of these processes. When done correctly, a key controls process enables you to embed the process with the process owners who will maintain the process documentation. A self-assessment questionnaire approach will probably not create adequate internal control process documentation.

The 2nd Best Reason Is:

Companies need an internal control review methodology that is based on an ongoing:

1. Key control comparison against established control standards.
2. Control deficiency identification, mitigation, and reporting process.
3. Control environment risk self-assessment and management process.
4. Maintenance of detailed control process design and control operation review/testing documentation.
5. Approach that prevents unwanted financial market surprises.
6. Methodology that will accomplish all of this at a reasonable cost and produce the most return for invested capital.

These are the primary reasons for management to want to develop a key controls methodology.

And the Best Reason Is:

The best reason to develop a key controls process is not and should not be purely compliance. It should be because it is a good management practice. A key controls process is a very good management practice, as you will learn in the next few chapters. For now, rest assured that if you are looking for the best internal control review process that will ensure compliance with all of the requirements we have reviewed thus far, and will do this at the least cost in the long-term, then please read on because the key controls process is the one for you.

CHAPTER 3
THE KEY CONTROLS PROCESS

> **"Quality is doing the right things, the right way,
> the first time, every time."**
> — Anonymous

Key Controls Definition

After reading the first chapter, you are familiar with the concepts of internal control. After reading the second chapter, you should understand why you probably need a better internal control evaluation process. The next step is to develop an understanding of key controls.

Key controls are those significant controls within our business processes, which if operating correctly will both ensure and give assurance that the organization is achieving its key business objectives.

As we learned in the first chapter, management designs and implements controls to control the work that is performed so they can minimize the risk of bad things happening. Based on the specific process that they are attempting to control and the control objectives that need to be achieved, many different controls and combinations of controls can be used. However, the one certainty is that management must design appropriate controls based on the risks that exist and therefore the control objectives that need to be achieved to adequately minimize these risks.

Within the set of controls that management designs to mitigate the inherent process risks are a set of significant controls, which are usually a subset of the total set of controls. If these controls are operating as designed and are adequately mitigating the inherent process risks, they will both ensure and give assurance to management that the organization is achieving its specific business process control objectives. And, if this is occurring for all significant business processes, then this organization is able to both ensure and give assurance to upper management that it is achieving its key business objectives.

Control Objectives

We explained control objectives in Chapter 1. However, following is a quick refresher of the typical generic control objectives for a financial process. Many different listings exist depending on the specific business process and whether it is an operational, financial, or compliance area:

- **Authorization** — Transactions are appropriately authorized by management.
- **Accuracy** — Transactions are properly calculated.
- **Valuation** — Appropriate measurement and recognition principles are applied.
- **Completeness** — All valid transactions are recorded.
- **Classification** — Transactions are properly classified.
- **Existence** — Recorded transactions actually occurred and were recorded only once.
- **Timeliness/cutoff** — Transactions are recorded in the correct period.
- **Safeguard assets** — Assets are secured from theft, damage, and unauthorized access or usage.
- **Segregation of duties** — Appropriate segregation between the authorization of transactions, the recording of transactions, and the maintenance of assets.

Control objectives enable the achievement of our **key business objectives:**

- Any process must be controlled to ensure desired results are achieved continually over time in an efficient and effective manner.
- Control objectives enable us to understand the controls that are needed.

When they are appropriately used, control objectives enable management to determine the specific controls that are needed to mitigate the inherent business risks within the business processes for which they are responsible. Therefore, control objectives enable management to achieve their key business objectives.

Business Objectives

Every organization has one or more key business objectives. For example, an accounting organization may have as its key business objective to:

> Provide accurate financial information that complies with management and regulatory requirements in an efficient, effective, and timely manner.

Now that we have discussed key controls, what all of the elements are, and how they fit together, it all comes together in the assurance structure. In other words, the assurance structure is how each of these elements fits together to ensure that management is able to achieve their business objectives.

```
┌─────────────────────────────────────────────────────────────────┐
│   ┌─────────────────────────────────────────────────┐           │
│   │      Assurance Structure & Key Controls          │           │
│   └─────────────────────────────────────────────────┘           │
│                                                                   │
│     Management's    Key Controls are:                             │
│      Business                                                     │
│      Objectives     – Significant controls within our            │
│                        business processes                         │
│      Business                                                     │
│      Process        – Which if operating correctly                │
│      Control                                                      │
│      Objectives     – Will both ensure and give                   │
│                        assurance                                  │
│      Key                                                          │
│      Controls       – That management is achieving its            │
│     (which are a       key business objectives                    │
│      subset of                                                    │
│      Control                                                      │
│      Activities)                                                  │
│                                                                   │
└─────────────────────────────────────────────────────────────────┘
```

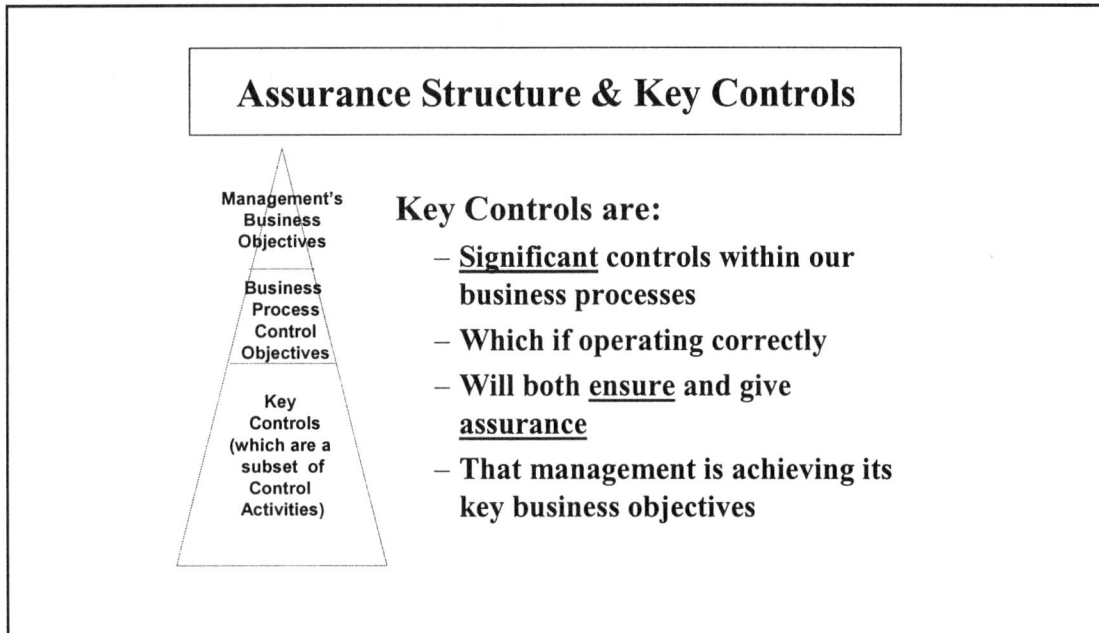

The pyramid demonstrates how key controls support the achievement of business process control objectives and how the achievement of business process control objectives then supports the achievement of management's business objectives. This is what we term the assurance structure.

Key Controls Process Objective

The objective of management in the design of a key controls process should be to identify the smallest number possible of key controls to be reviewed that will enable management to:

- Ensure and give assurance that control objectives are achieved.
- Ensure that its overall business objectives are being achieved.

Why have the smallest possible number of key controls? It is because of the cost benefit struggle that management always faces in designing controls. The objective is to get the most benefit for the least cost, and it costs money to review key controls. Therefore, you want to design as efficient and effective a system of review as possible.

Key Controls is a Quality Control and Assurance Process

The key controls process is a quality control and assurance process for internal control processes. The author's preferred definition of quality is:

Doing the right things, the right way, the first time, every time.

Key controls are actually quality control points established within our internal control process. These control points are established in the process where management needs assurance that process control objectives are achieved. In order to ensure that control objectives are achieved consistently, quality standards are established for each key control. These quality standards are based on the minimum level of acceptable quality that must be achieved to ensure control objectives are achieved. Quality control points (key controls) and minimum standards of control (quality standards for each key control) are the most basic and important components of a key controls process. It is the appropriate determination and establishment of key controls and minimum standards of control, and once established, the appropriate review of these elements that is most critical in ensuring a successful key controls process.

The Ongoing Process

The key controls process is an ongoing self-audit process. Although it is based on self-assessment, as we discussed previously, most self-assessment processes are based on knowledge rather than on the testing of key controls against minimum standards of control.

Key controls processes, as explained in this text, are an ongoing self-audit process because the personnel responsible for reviewing key controls are responsible for ensuring that the key control is verified against the established minimum standard based on a required review schedule. The actual review must be based on appropriate evidence of control, which must be:

- Complete and accurate.
- Appropriately reviewed and approved.
- Sufficient evidence upon which to base and support the conclusions reached.
- Appropriately maintained.

These personnel are also responsible for ensuring that all exceptions to achieve the minimum standard of control for a given key control are appropriately mitigated and reported. For all exceptions to achieve the minimum standard of control established, the responsible personnel must determine and submit on a timely basis:

- A description of the control exception.
- A proposed resolution.

- A proposed resolution estimated time line.
- An estimate of the financial impact resulting from the exception.

If the financial impact resulting from the exception is potentially significant, then an explanation must be provided as to why the submitting organization is able to conclude that its financial statements are stated in accordance with generally accepted accounting principles (GAAP).

It should be understood that management is not to report internal control deficiencies. Rather management is required to adhere to the principles enumerated and to report internal control weaknesses that are appropriately mitigated. As part of the key controls process, management is also required to supply appropriate certifications for their areas of responsibility in which they give assurance that our control objectives are being achieved.

Key Controls is an Ongoing Risk Assessment and Reporting Process

Integrated into the key controls process is an ongoing risk assessment and reporting process. This process, which we call the "Significant Events and Judgments Process," is intended to enable management to:

- Continually assess the risks that occur and have potential impact upon their areas of responsibility.
- Be able to report these risks up through the chain of command to ensure all levels are appropriately advised of these risks.
- Ensure that these risks are appropriately mitigated.

CHAPTER 4
DEVELOPING KEY CONTROLS

> "In theory, there is no difference between theory and practice.
> But, in practice, there is."
> — Jan L.A. van de Snepscheut

It is important to understand that a key controls process is based on responsibility. Each manager must own the key controls for his or her areas of responsibility. It is also important to understand that one of the areas of greatest risk and control failure can be the interfaces or hand-offs that exist between owners and their processes. Therefore, in determining responsibilities for controls in each of these areas, one must also review the responsibility between areas and ensure that one area is clearly responsible.

As with any internal controls process review, in developing key controls processes, one must begin with control objectives. There was a reason control objectives were the first concept covered in this book and are now being discussed for at least the third time. The achievement of control objectives is the fundamental objective of any system of internal control, and key controls are simply another internal control process.

Control Objectives — The Starting Point

The first and certainly one of the most important steps in developing a set of key controls for any business process is to determine the control objectives for each activity. Therefore, the first step on our journey is to:

1. Determine the **control objectives** that must be achieved to ensure our **business objectives** are realized for a specific process activity, financial cycle, or account balance.

For any given process, activity, or account balance, management has specific control objectives — the objectives of management that are derived from the desire to protect themselves from the risks inherent within any business process. A valid approach to developing control objectives for an activity, process, or account balance is to determine and review the risks for what could go wrong. For example, in any specific process, activity, or account balance there is a risk that expenditures would not be appropriately authorized in compliance with management's criteria. To develop the control objective based on this risk, turn it around and the control objective becomes to ensure that all expenditures are appropriately authorized in accordance with management's criteria.

In Chapter 1, we reviewed a list of generic control objectives that will fit well as a starting point for most financial activities. As a reminder, here again are the set of financial control objectives that we discussed previously:

- **Authorization** — Transactions are appropriately authorized by management.
- **Accuracy** — Transactions are properly calculated.
- **Valuation** — Appropriate measurement and recognition principles are applied.
- **Completeness** — All valid transactions are recorded.
- **Classification** — Transactions are properly classified.
- **Existence** — Recorded transactions actually occurred and were recorded only once.
- **Timeliness/cutoff** — Transactions are recorded in the correct period.
- **Safeguard assets** — Assets are secured from theft, damage, and unauthorized access or usage.
- **Segregation of duties** — Appropriate segregation between the authorization of transactions, the recording of transactions, and the maintenance of assets.

We should also note that within the safeguarding of assets control objective, there is a **Records Retention** control objective. This should not be overlooked.

However, there is a serious problem with this set of generic control objectives — no one set can fit every situation. According to COSO's definition, internal control is a process designed to provide reasonable assurance to management of the achievement of control objectives in the following three categories of control:

- Effectiveness and efficiency of operations.
- Reliability of financial reporting.
- Compliance with applicable laws and regulations.

Management has an objective to ensure the efficiency and effectiveness of operations, and to ensure compliance with applicable laws and regulations. Note that neither of these objective categories is listed in the generic control objectives above. In addition, although the objectives listed above are generic financial control objectives, one of the most important was not listed — **Adequate Disclosure**. This control objective must be achieved to ensure reliable financial reporting.

As we learned in Chapter 2, the Sarbanes-Oxley Act under Section 302 requires the registrant's chief executive and financial officers to certify that they have ensured adequate financial disclosure. Moreover, there are many other disclosure requirements in generally accepted accounting principles (GAAP) and within the SEC's disclosure rules with which a registrant must comply. However, this objective is missing from the list above, and the reason again is that generic listings of control objectives are only a starting point. The problem with generic listings is that for any specific process or activity or even account balance, they are simply too generic.

Since our objective is actually to determine the controls that are needed, customized control objectives, which are specific to the area under review, are a big help. They save time — a lot of time. If you use generic control objectives as your starting point, then you are going to need much more experienced and capable personnel to be able to determine the internal control activities that are required to achieve these objectives. This is because a high level of internal control review knowledge and experience is necessary to be able to use generic control objectives to determine the right set of controls that are needed to achieve them. Therefore, the second step in the process of developing key controls is to:

2. **Customize** the generic control objectives to be specific to the control process, activity, cycle, or account.

In a revenue cycle, activity, or account there is always a generic authorization control objective that:

Transactions are appropriately authorized in accordance with management's criteria.

What types of transactions in a revenue activity need to be appropriately authorized? If the control objective were customized to a revenue area, it would read more like the following:

Customers are approved for service according to management's criteria based on credit worthiness.

This is a revenue specific control objective. It is specific to a revenue area that has significant transactions in dollar amount where the credit worthiness of customers is important. Because the control objective is customized, it gives the person who is trying to determine the controls necessary to achieve this control objective much better information with which to work. In other words, if you knew the exact business activity and account for which this is an objective, you would have a much easier time determining the internal control activities that are needed to achieve the objective. This is why the customization of control objectives is so important. It saves time and money. Less experienced personnel can use the above control objective to determine the right set of controls than is required if we begin with and use the generic objective. However, do not lead the witness by listing desired controls.

Sometimes control objectives are too customized. In fact, they can be so customized that they are no longer really control objectives. For example:

Does the automated process have adequate hash, batch, and record counts?

The above is supposed to be a control objective; however, it is not. Instead, it is asking whether specific controls exist in an automated process. This leading of the witness should be avoided because it causes the reviewer to determine if these specific controls exist and to conclude that if they do, everything is all right. The problem is that these controls may or may not be adequate to ensure the achievement of the control objectives. You want to use control objectives that enable the user to understand what the objective is and what types of controls are needed to achieve the objective without leading the user to search for specific controls. The types of controls that exist are not the most important factor here. What is most important is that the controls taken as a whole adequately mitigate the risk, achieving the control objective at reasonable cost. There is considerable judgment involved in this process, and you want to facilitate this analysis as much as possible without leading the reviewer to a wrong conclusion.

Guidance

This is not to say that you cannot or should not use guidance. Guidance is usually a set of instructions that explains the types of controls that generally exist within the area. This guidance can be and usually is very useful in that it enables the understanding of the reviewer as to what to look for in relation to controls. Moreover, it does not mislead the reviewer because he or she is still required to identify an adequate set of controls to achieve the control objectives.

Customized Control Objectives

So, where do you get customized control objectives? First, you can develop them yourself. You can begin with the generic control objectives mentioned above for any activity. By developing an understanding of the activity, you can develop customized control objectives. However, this takes time, experience, and ability. In fact, if attempting this approach, it is recommended that you utilize internal control review specialists to develop the customized control objectives. They could come from your internal audit department or an appropriate vendor.

Second, there are vendors that have developed customized control objectives. However, even vendor-supplied customized control objectives will probably require some additional customization due to the uniqueness of your company and its specific processes and circumstances. Nevertheless, you may find that the time and related cost you save in purchasing customized control objectives may well outweigh the cost. It will depend on how well the customized control objectives fit your business processes.

Third, the COSO internal control framework has control objectives included as a resource within the tools that were published. This is an excellent source of customized control objectives. However, the COSO objectives probably are not as customized to specific business processes, activities, and account balances as the control objectives that a third-party vendor could supply.

Review and Documentation Processes

Once the control objectives for a given business process have been identified, the next step is to review and document the process. This is usually done in either a narrative or a flowchart format.

There are lots of different formats, tools, and approaches that can be used. Since any large company will usually have an existing approach that works, it is assumed that your company has a methodology that works and that your external auditor is satisfied with it. If your external auditors have not signed off on your review and documentation methodology, then you might want to review it with them, because one that is not a good fit for your external auditor will take longer and cost more to review, and could lead to errors in interpretation leading to lengthy discussions — all of which is inefficient and should be avoided.

The most important point to understand in this step is that our intent is only to develop such documentation so that we can identify and understand the controls that exist currently in the business process. Here is where the greatest amount of inefficiency can exist in developing key controls, because as any experienced internal control reviewer knows, inexperienced reviewers tend to get too absorbed in learning how to document. They tend to believe that documenting is the end in itself and not just a means to an entirely different end. This seems to be because it is easy to document, you are being paid to document, and you can do a really good job of documenting a business process. You can document every intricate detail. However, this is not and never will be the objective. The objective is to minimize this step as much as possible.

The only reason to document the business process is to identify the controls that exist within it, and we are not interested in all of the controls — just those that we will rely upon to ensure the achievement of the control objectives. For example, everyone budgets. Budgeting is an important process. However, unless you are actually reviewing the budgeting process, you will probably never be relying on budgeting to achieve your control objectives. Since we are primarily concerned with internal control over financial reporting, budgeting is probably not a significant process in any of the areas that we would review. Therefore, a detailed explanation of this process should not show up in our process documentation. However, I know that I detailed this process rather well in a review that I performed early in my own career. At the time, I felt it was important to do so because I wanted to do a thorough job of documenting the area.

It should probably be mentioned that inexperienced internal control reviewers also have a tendency to list too many controls for each control objective. Only the significant controls that will be relied upon to achieve the control objectives should be listed. Again, budgeting probably will never be listed. Therefore, step three is to:

3. Review and document key processes.

   • Processes are normally documented in process flow flowcharts or narratives

Step four is:

4. The identification of controls to be relied upon.

- Many controls usually exist, but only list the ones that will be relied upon to achieve the control objective.
- Valid controls such as budgeting and forecasting controls should be excluded.

The Search for Missing Controls

Now that we have identified the control objectives for our business activity and the internal control activities that currently exist, our next step would normally be to document this information in a control matrix — a spreadsheet with columns. The first column is used to list all of the control objectives for the business activity being reviewed. The second column is generally used to list the internal control activities that we identified in the third and fourth steps above. The objective now is to compare control objectives against the identified internal control activities and determine if any required internal control activities necessary to achieve the control objectives are missing.

This is an important step. In fact, it is one of the most important steps in the entire process because this is where you determine if there are actually enough controls in place to achieve the control objectives. This is where you determine the adequacy of control design. For example, a modern general ledger system will usually have a detailed listing or table of all accounting transactions. It will also have a ledger table in which a single balance is maintained for each business unit, department, account, and other chart field. This modern ledger table is no more than an automated paper ledger. Due to the size of the ledger table, many modern automated general ledger systems will have summary ledgers. Summary ledgers are an automated summarization of the ledger table. However, they do not have all of the detail of the ledger table and are therefore more efficient for reporting.

Summary ledgers must be complete and accurate summarizations of the detailed ledger table. If this control objective is not achieved, then our external financial reporting will be as inaccurate as the summary ledgers. How could the summary ledger table not be complete and accurate? In any automated summarization process, there should be controls to ensure that all transactions are completely and accurately summarized. However, it is possible for a summarization job to end abnormally — and for no one to know. For example, the job used to process the summary ledger could have ended normally on a job step before the process was completed. Since there is a risk that the summary ledger could be inaccurate and be relied upon for external financial reporting, there must be a method or control that can be relied upon to ensure the completeness and accuracy of the summary ledgers.

An example of a control that will appropriately mitigate this risk is to develop an automated process that will recalculate the summarization of the detailed ledger. This job will produce the same result as one that was used to create the summary ledger. The independent results of this verification job are then compared to the actual process so that the complete and accurate processing of the summary table can be confirmed. If this control is missing, there is always the potential that your summary ledgers are inaccurate and you do not know it. Therefore, if this control were not present for your general ledger system, you would have a missing internal control activity that is necessary to ensure your financial reporting is complete and accurate and the process control objectives are achieved. This would be an internal control design deficiency.

A manual control can also be used to achieve this same end. Any control or combination of controls can be used to achieve a control objective. In many situations, it does not matter whether manual or automated controls are utilized as long as the control objectives are achieved. When the costs versus the benefits of certain controls are considered, many times automated controls are preferred, but this is generally a cost efficiency issue — not a control adequacy issue.

If a control activity is missing, then there is an internal control design deficiency and management must determine a plan to resolve this control weakness.

Therefore, step five is to:

5.   Search for missing controls.

- Enough controls must be identified for each control objective to ensure it is adequately achieved.
- If enough controls are not in place to ensure control objective achievement, then a control is missing.
- Plans to develop missing controls and mitigate the control weakness must be developed.

Test Identified Controls

When the controls that were identified as being in place are added to those that were identified as missing, we should have sufficient controls to achieve the control objectives. However, one cannot just assume the controls that were determined to be in place are operating as designed. They must be tested. There have been many times when someone told an auditor that the controls they expected to find were present and working, just to find out that these controls were either nonexistent or nonfunctioning when tested.

In their final rules on Sarbanes-Oxley Section 404, the SEC stated the following in relation to required testing of internal control over financial reporting and the development and retention of evidential matter:

The assessment of a company's internal control over financial reporting must be based on procedures sufficient both to evaluate its design and to test its operating effectiveness. Controls subject to such assessment include, but are not limited to: controls over initiating, recording, processing and reconciling account balances, classes of transactions and disclosure and related assertions included in the financial statements; controls related to the initiation and processing of non-routine and non-systematic transactions; controls related to the selection and application of appropriate accounting policies; and controls related to the prevention, identification, and detection of fraud. The nature of a company's testing activities will largely depend on the circumstances of the company and the significance of the control. However, inquiry alone generally will not provide an adequate basis for management's assessment.

An assessment of the effectiveness of internal control over financial reporting must be supported by evidential matter, including documentation, regarding both the design of internal controls and the testing processes. This evidential matter should provide reasonable support: for the evaluation of whether the control is designed to prevent or detect material misstatements or omissions; for the conclusion that the tests were appropriately planned and performed; and that the results of the tests were appropriately considered. The public accounting firm that is required to attest to, and report on, management's assessment of the effectiveness of the company's internal control over financial reporting also will require that the company develop and maintain such evidential matter to support management's assessment.

My favorite quote from the PCAOB's discussion of their proposed auditing standard is, "The proposed standard would allow the auditor to use, to a reasonable degree, the work performed by others, including management. Thus, the more extensive and reliable management's assessment is, the less extensive and costly the auditor's work will need to be."

An external auditor cannot rely upon management's testing as the only evidence that controls are operating as designed. However, they can decrease the amount of testing they perform, and the cost to you, if they are comfortable with the testing you performed. Therefore, if you want your external auditors to reduce the amount of testing they perform based on your test work, you will need to ensure that you use testing procedures that they can rely upon — and all reliance on your test work should save you money.

Where the test results show that the controls tested are not operating as designed, management must develop adequate plans to resolve these issues so that the control objectives will be adequately achieved. Therefore, step six is:

6. Test identified controls (control activities) that will be relied upon to achieve control objectives.

    *   Reasonable tests must be performed of these controls to prove that they are operating as designed.
    *   Management must develop plans to address controls that are not working as designed.

Determine Key Controls

Up to this point, you will have used a very traditional approach to the review of internal controls. An internal auditor would usually stop at this point, as he or she has completed the "normal" internal control review process. The auditor would next write up the control weaknesses (deficiencies) that were identified for missing and nonoperating controls and, after a lot of editing, issue a report. However, here is actually where we begin our development of key controls. In reality, you do not have to go through all of the prior process. However, given the fact that you really want to build a good system, and you want your external auditor to feel comfortable in relying upon it, you really should.

For the purposes of this exercise, let us assume that we have reviewed an activity, process, cycle, or account using the above-enumerated methodology. Given these parameters, one would review the set of internal controls that were identified and determine which of these controls should be key controls. It really is that simple — or is it? Key controls are usually not all of the controls that were identified. They are the most significant of the controls, which can be relied upon such that, when taken as a whole, they can both ensure and give assurance that the control objectives are adequately achieved, and therefore that the organization is achieving its key business objectives.

For example, in a journal entry process, there are a large number of controls that ensure the complete, accurate, and timely completion of journal entries. There are:

- Assigned, usually sequential, journal entry numbers.
- Input edits on valid company, department, account, and other general ledger classification parameters.
- Separate journal entry review and approval that includes a manual confirmation that the journal documentation is adequate.
- Closing schedule and process to ensure journal entries are booked in appropriate sequence.
- Journal entry listings that are checked to ensure all expected, required journal entries are completed before the accounting period is closed.

These are just a few of the controls. There are actually a lot more depending on how you break them down. However, these are the primary controls you would probably list on a control matrix in order to be able to ensure the control objectives are achieved for the journal entry process. Given all of these controls, which are or should be key controls? What happens if we only use the last control listed above as our key control?

If we want to ensure and to give assurance to management that the process control objectives are being adequately achieved and the organization is meeting its key business objectives, can we assume that reviewing just the journal entry sign-off sheets on an ongoing monthly basis is sufficient to ensure that all journal entries were prepared timely, accurately, and completely? I believe we can, and the reason is that most of the other controls had to have worked in this area for us to be able to have gotten all of the journal entries entered on time. Moreover, let us not forget the review we just performed above of the entire journal entry process. During this review, we reviewed each of these controls and determined that they were operating as designed. Once in place, most of these controls continue to operate as designed (for example, journal entry numbering). Once the usage of unique journal entry numbers is established, this process tends to continue. In addition, we intend to review this process again next year and update this understanding. Therefore, on an ongoing monthly basis, can we only review the journal entry listing to both ensure and give assurance to management that process control objectives are being achieved and the organization is achieving its key business objectives? If we can, then it is because the other controls in the journal entry process can be relied upon to work as designed, if we review and validate that the journal entry listing control is operating as designed.

The concept of key controls is that only some of the controls in place need to be validated on a more frequent basis in order to achieve adequate assurance that all of the process control objectives are adequately being achieved and the organization is achieving its key business objectives.

If major process changes occur during the year, then we should perform a detailed review of these areas. However, most control activities tend to operate as designed for at least a year, and to comply with Sarbanes-Oxley Section 404 requirements, we intend to review all internal control over financial reporting annually. Internal audit will also review compliance and operational areas on an ongoing risk-based cycle. Therefore, it is reasonable for management to use a key controls-based approach to achieve ongoing assurance as to the effective operation of internal control. Key controls that are part of the company's disclosure controls and procedures can also be used on an ongoing basis to give reasonable assurance that the company's disclosure controls and procedures are effective.

Another of the controls above will probably be an ongoing monthly key control. In the general ledger table and security maintenance area of the company, someone is responsible for setting up general ledger system input edits. That person will probably have a key control, which will be to ensure that all general ledger system input edit maintenance is done in a complete, accurate, and timely manner. On an ongoing, monthly basis, two different areas — accounting and system processing — would have two different key controls based on their responsibilities. These controls would enable management to ensure and give assurance to upper management, the audit committee, and the board of directors that the control objectives for the journal entry process are being achieved.

In theory, you should attempt to identify as few key controls as possible that will ensure the control objectives are achieved. However, in practice, I suggest you ensure that your external auditor is comfortable with the key controls identified. This is another reason the approach enumerated above should be used.

Types of Controls: Preventative, Detective, and Corrective

Another point is that the key controls you identify will tend to be more detective and corrective in nature than preventative. One way of looking at controls is to view them from the perspective of how they work.

Preventative Controls

Preventative controls are generally your best controls. This is because they prevent mistakes from being made and the cost of correcting mistakes. They usually are automated and work 24/7. Once you design, implement, and pay for them, they tend to be in place and operate correctly all of the time. This is because these controls tend to work (unless something changes), and generally do not need to be reviewed regularly to ensure they are reliable. Therefore, preventative controls are generally the best type of controls because they prevent mistakes.

To illustrate, journal entry input edits are preventative controls. They are automated and work 24/7. Any time the journal entry system is operating and accepting journal entries, the input edits should be working and operating consistently as designed. It is best to prevent mistakes and rework because it is better to prevent an error from occurring than to have to pay to fix it. Since preventative controls prevent errors from occurring, they are the best type of controls.

However, it is critical that the control maintenance that is performed on these controls be performed in a complete and accurate manner. Therefore, although automated preventative controls will usually not be identified as key controls that need to be reviewed on an ongoing basis, the maintenance performed on automated preventative controls needs to have appropriate key controls established that need to be monitored on an ongoing basis. In other words, a key control should be established to review the maintenance performed on automated preventative controls to ensure these changes are reliable, since the maintenance is a manual process.

Detective Controls

Detective controls are not as good as preventative controls because, although they detect errors in time to be fixed, the errors still must be fixed. Therefore, a correction must be made. Detective controls do enable one to find the error and correct it before the books are misstated — or before other such consequences are incurred.

Even though many controls can be automated, a lot more cannot. A journal entry that passes the input edits still needs to be reviewed and approved. For example, the debit and credit may get reversed, which is something automated input edits cannot determine. Additionally, a reviewer needs to review the journal entry documentation and ensure that it is adequate enough to *"stand on its own"* — meaning that, for example, five years later in a tax audit, a tax auditor should be able to pull a journal entry and understand it completely. After reviewing the journal entry, the tax auditor should not end up wishing there was someone who could explain it. Such an occurrence would probably lead the tax auditor to assume whatever was in the best interest of the taxing authority. The reason the journal entry review is a detective control is that if the review is performed appropriately, then any errors will be detected and can be corrected before the journal is posted in error.

Corrective Controls

Corrective controls are the least efficient because they are not performed before the error is made and finalized. They allow you to correct an error; however, there is a cost to the error that was not prevented or detected timely that must now be paid. For example, account reconciliation is an excellent corrective control. It is a very important control that is used to identify many minor accounting, mainly misclassification, errors. However, account reconciliations are not normally completed until after the books are closed and the financial statements issued. Therefore, account reconciliations are a corrective control. However, if the account reconciliation is completed and any identified errors are posted to the books of record before the books are closed for the period, then the account reconciliation becomes a detective control. Whether an internal control is detective or corrective can be dependent upon whether it is completed before or after the closing of the books of record.

Corrective controls tend to be the most expensive for several reasons. For example, for account reconciliations, one reason is that the books are wrong based on whatever accounting errors were made that the reconciliations are going to eventually find. Second, the books tend to stay wrong for the period of time that it takes to complete the reconciliations. Third, you would not have to do account reconciliations if the preventative and corrective controls had worked. In fact, that is exactly why you want to concentrate your money and effort on building the best preventative and then detective controls you can. These controls cost the least and work the best.

The account reconciliation verifies whether the preventative and detective controls are working, and how well they are working. Additionally, when the reconciliation is completed, if it is done correctly, then you know that the account balance is correct. However, one does not want to be surprised by how many of the account reconciliations scheduled to be completed were not completed. This is why corrective controls tend to be key controls that are validated on an ongoing monthly basis. One can wait and review these quarterly; however, if one does, one may be surprised by how far behind and how much work is now necessary to ensure adequate control. This is not only because a large volume of reconciliations may not be completed timely, but also because a nonfunctioning preventative or detective control may have caused a large volume of errors that will not be determined until the reconciliations are completed.

Depending on the circumstances, processes, and automated systems in place, controls can vary between being preventative, detective, and corrective. As a summary of the above discussion, the key controls in a journal entry system would probably be:

Preventative:

- Chart field entity and combination input edits (key control of the maintenance support function)

Detective:

- Journal entry review and approval (only if not automated and required)
- Checklist of journal entries for the period (always required because of nonrecurring onetime journal entries)

Corrective:

- Account reconciliation (always required because one generally has errors that can only be corrected via the reconciliation process)

Analytical Review

Another control that is usually not identified and reviewed as a key control (but is one of the most important) is analytical review. It is usually the last line against accounting misstatements since it usually occurs after almost all accounting entries are made for the period and just prior to the closing of the books. To perform analytical reviews, companies generally develop formalized income and balance sheet account reviews where the current period balances are reviewed against various prior period, budget, and projection amounts to determine variances that should be reviewed and explained. This control is based on the experience and knowledge of management. It is the ability to review financial statements and pick out areas that do not look "right" for further review (based on an understanding of the business) and what the financials should reflect (based on an understanding of the relationships between accounts). Many errors can transverse the gambit of existing preventative and detective controls without detection to be found by the last detective control — analytical review. The importance of this control cannot be understated.

In Chapter 2, we quoted the PCAOB's proposed auditing standard which stated that the identification of a material misstatement in the current period's financial statements by the external auditor that was not initially identified by the company's internal control over financial reporting "should be regarded as at least a significant deficiency and is a strong indicator that a material weakness in internal control over financial reporting exists." This position should be avoided if at all possible, since company management in such a situation would have a difficult and potentially unsuccessful time convincing the external auditor that such an occurrence was not a material weakness. The overall internal control over financial reporting must, of course, be sufficient and effective to avoid this situation. However, the company must have adequate analytical review procedures to ensure that any large transactions that are not recorded during the normal course of business are caught during the analytical review procedures and are recorded timely.

Consistency of Control Quality

Another of the issues related to key controls is ensuring consistent quality. Not all account reconciliations need to be performed using the exact same procedures. However, a consistent quality of control should be achieved for all reconciliations performed, and this is the subject of our next chapter.

Therefore, step seven is:

7. Determine the key controls that, when taken as a whole, can both ensure and give assurance that the control objectives are adequately achieved and, therefore, key business objectives are achieved.

- Key controls are not all of the controls identified.
- They must provide adequate evidence that the control objectives were achieved.
- Key controls tend to be more detective and corrective than preventative.

CHAPTER 5
THE MINIMUM STANDARD
OF CONTROL

> **"Quality is never an accident; it is always the result of high intention, sincere effort, intelligent direction, and skillful execution; it represents the wise choice of many alternatives."**
> **— William A. Foster**

The Minimum Standard of Control

As we learned in the last chapter, the "right" key controls to verify a specific process will depend on the specifics of that process. The "right" key controls for similar areas within a single company may differ. However, management should always ensure that a consistent level of control quality is achieved equally for all processes. For example, in a medium-sized company, many different accounting departments will perform account reconciliations for the accounts they own. The available staff, the dollar volume of transactions flowing through the accounts, the absolute dollar size of the account balances, and the type of accounts can all affect the reconciliation procedures used. However, for all account reconciliations, management should seek to obtain a "consistent quality of control." The exact same reconciliation procedures, such as review and approval, may differ based on many factors. But a reasonable standard must be determined and enforced to ensure consistent quality of control. This standard that is established against which actual performance is compared is called the "minimum standard of control." A minimum standard of control must be determined and established for each key control, and together the key control and its minimum standard are the two most fundamental and important components of the key controls process.

Developing Minimum Standards of Control

If you have identified all the correct key controls, and therefore all of the quality points that need to be checked to be able to give assurance that an appropriate level of quality will be achieved for a given process, you will need to develop minimum standards of control that will ensure each quality point (key control) was achieved to the right level of quality.

To assist in understanding this concept, let us compare a traditional checklist item such as one for bank account reconciliation to a well-formulated key control and minimum standard of control.

The checklist item would say: Completed bank account XYZ reconciliation.

The key control and minimum standard would say:

Monthly - Key Control	**Minimum Standard of Control**
Reconciliation of XYZ Account	Within 30 days of receipt of the bank statement, the bank account was reconciled to an immaterial difference. All identified adjustments were reviewed, approved, and posted.

The difference is that the minimum standard of control requires that a specific level of quality be achieved, such as:

1. The minimum standard is specific as to the timing of when the bank account must be reconciled. It specifically requires that the account be reconciled within 30 days of receipt of the bank statement and that the reconciliation be performed monthly.

2. The minimum standard specifically requires that the bank account be reconciled to an immaterial difference. Although this allows for appropriate judgment, it is specific to ensure that it is understood that a large unreconciled difference is not appropriate.

3. The minimum standard specifically requires that any identified adjustments be reviewed, approved, and posted. This is because there is a risk that the bank account could be reconciled to an immaterial difference monthly, but the adjustments would only be tracked in the reconciliation and not be posted to the books of record. This last requirement is intended to ensure the bank account is adjusted appropriately in the accounting records.

Minimum Standards of Control and Control Objectives

Minimum standards of control should ensure that the key control is completed in a manner that achieves our control objectives in a complete, timely, and accurate manner. Therefore, minimum standards of control are actually related to the control objectives that the key control is attempting to achieve. In fact, when properly formulated, minimum standards are derived based on the control failure risks that the key control is attempting to prevent.

Let's review our minimum standard for the bank reconciliation from this perspective. In our minimum standard of control, there are three fundamental elements that must be achieved:

Minimum Standard of Control

1. Within 30 days of receipt of the bank statement,
2. The bank account was reconciled to an immaterial difference,
3. All identified adjustments were reviewed, approved, and posted.

The three items above comprise a standard intended to prevent the three major mistakes that can be made while completing a bank account reconciliation. These mistakes are the three major risks of control failure. Therefore, any bank reconciliation should be reviewed to ensure that these mistakes are not made (i.e., reasonable quality is achieved).

The first mistake is not reconciling the bank statement timely. You will remember that **timeliness/ cutoff** was one of the basic control objectives discussed earlier. In this instance, the timeliness control objective would be to "ensure that the bank account is reconciled in a timely manner in accordance with management's criteria." This is, of course, a customization of the generic objective discussed in Chapter 4.

For bank accounts, there is a need to perform an account reconciliation timely because banks typically have an adjustment period in their bank account agreements which states that they will accept and make adjustments to the account that the company brings to their attention for a period of only 45 to 60 days after the bank statement is issued. After this adjustment period ends, no adjustments in favor of the company will be made. Adjustments in favor of the bank will, however, be accepted and made at anytime. So, there is a risk that if bank account adjustments are not determined timely and communicated to the bank, the bank may refuse to make them. Therefore, bank accounts need to be reconciled timely.

The second mistake is not performing the reconciliation accurately. You should also remember that **accuracy** was one of our basic control objectives. Again, for a bank account reconciliation, a customization of the generic accuracy control objective is required. While the generic accuracy objective was that transactions are properly calculated, the specific, customized bank account reconciliation control objective should be something such as all account adjustments must be appropriately determined.

Failure to achieve this control objective occurs when certain unmatched items are not researched and matched against other items, or other differences between the bank's and the company's account balances are left unresolved, such as recording bank fees. The component of the minimum standard of control that is established to prevent this risk as stated above is that the account should be reconciled to an immaterial difference. In accounting terms, this means that the reconciler must research and resolve all significant differences between the bank's and the company's account balances. It also means that both balances must be adjusted appropriately until they are reasonably close based on an appropriate application of materiality. A plug, or an undetermined amount, cannot be added or subtracted from the company's bank account balance in order to agree it or balance it to the bank's balance. This accounting reconciliation theory is implied by the simple statement that is made as the second part of the minimum standard of control, and this statement should be sufficient to ensure that the accuracy control objective is achieved.

The third mistake or risk of control failure is that all of the necessary adjustments required to reconcile the company's account balance to the bank's account balance will be determined; however, no adjustments will be entered into the accounting system. The control objective that attempts to control this risk is the **completeness** objective. In this case, the generic objective of ensuring that all valid transactions were recorded would appear to fit. Of course, if the adjustments are not recorded as necessary to the company's account, then the company's bank account balance is not correct, and is not properly reconciled to the bank's account.

There is another control objective incorporated into the third requirement of the minimum standard: "All identified adjustments were reviewed, approved, and posted." Management should appropriately authorize all processing of transactions, which is our **authorization** objective. Achievement of this control objective is intended to mitigate the risk that transactions are not appropriately authorized, which is a risk in any transactions processing. One could have established a separate key control for this one objective. However, it was much more efficient and effective to incorporate this control objective into the minimum standard of control of the bank account reconciliation key control than it would have been to establish a separate key control.

There are other control objectives that are incorporated into this minimum standard of control, although it is not obvious. For example, the **valuation** control objective: "Appropriate measurement and recognition principles applied." This control objective is actually incorporated into two separate parts of the minimum standard of control. First, the requirement that "the bank account is reconciled to an immaterial difference" incorporates the concept that the differences determined will be valued correctly. Second, the requirement that "all identified adjustments were reviewed, approved, and posted" incorporates into it the concept that appropriate recognition principles were applied. In fact, the above minimum standard, without expressly addressing the **classification** and **existence** control objective, implies that these control objectives should be achieved. If you are required to identify adjustments as in the minimum standard of control above, then they should meet the existence control objective that "recorded transactions actually occurred and were recorded only once" and the classification control objective that "transactions are properly classified." Appropriate classification in this case would require that recorded adjustments be recorded to the appropriate bank account — as one side of the accounting adjustments — and to the appropriate income, expense, or other account — as the other side of the accounting entries.

It is important to note and recognize how a well-formulated minimum standard of control:

1. Ensures the appropriate completion of the key control, and
2. Achieves this by linking the appropriate completion of the key control directly to the control objectives that the key control is attempting to achieve.

Determination of Minimum Standards

How does one determine the minimum standard of control for a key control? One way is to know what the common control failures are for a key control and turn these into a standard. However, this requires a lot of experience. Just as one might miss identifying a necessary key control if not using an approach based on control objectives, the minimum standards of control might be missing necessary elements if not based on control objectives. The appropriate manner in which minimum standards of control should be developed is based on a review of the control objectives that the key control was developed to achieve. This means that key controls are determined from control objectives, and the minimum standards should also be derived from these same control objectives.

To derive appropriate minimum standards of control one should review each of the control objectives a key control is attempting to achieve and ask what specific criteria must be achieved for this key control to achieve each control objective. Appropriate criteria to achieve each control objective become part of the minimum standard of control. All of these criteria together become the minimum standard of control.

Mapping Key Controls

If you followed the approach detailed in Chapter 4 for developing key controls, your next step is going to be relatively easy. The process detailed in Chapter 4 should have enabled you to develop a control matrix for each process, activity, cycle, or account reviewed. This control matrix has for each process, activity, cycle, or account the relevant control objectives determined along with all of the control activities. Once you have this control matrix, you use it to determine the minimum standard of control for each key control. To illustrate, in the control matrix, we might expect the control activity "bank account reconciliation" to be listed several times under several different control objectives. Based on the categorization of controls as being preventative, detective, or corrective (as also discussed in Chapter 4), we know that a bank account reconciliation is generally a corrective control because it generally does not take place until after the books of record are closed for the period. Bank account reconciliations are necessary to ensure that our cash accounts are fairly stated and we know that it is important to keep these reconciliations current or we risk undesirable consequences. Therefore, the reconciliation of bank accounts is probably an ongoing monthly corrective key control.

It is very difficult to validate key controls using a control matrix on an ongoing basis. This is because a single control activity is usually listed under multiple control objectives. For example, the control activity bank account reconciliation could be listed under the timeliness/cutoff, accuracy, completeness, authorization, valuation, classification, and existence control objectives. However, we are only going to test this key control once each month to validate that it has achieved all of these control objectives. To do this in the most efficient and effective manner, one should list the bank account reconciliation key control once and then develop a minimum standard of control that appropriately incorporates all of the requirements necessary to ensure the achievement of all the required control objectives. Again, for our bank account reconciliation, the following is provided as an example:

The key control and minimum standard would say:

Monthly — Key Control	**Minimum Standard of Control**
Reconciliation of XYZ Account	Within 30 days of receipt of the bank statement, the bank account was reconciled to an immaterial difference. All identified adjustments were reviewed, approved, and posted.

Testing Key Controls

One would then test the bank account reconciliation key control against its minimum standard of review on an ongoing monthly basis. This monthly testing would probably be in the nature of validating that all of the required bank accounts were reconciled in compliance with the established minimum standard. If or when required, one could then map the completion of key controls to the multiple control objectives that they support to denote their achievement. A sufficient number of key controls would need to be determined and have appropriate minimum standards of control developed such that all of the process, activity, cycle, or account control objectives could be efficiently validated. Such that the ongoing monthly review of key controls would then support that the significant controls within our business processes were operating effectively and both ensure and give assurance that management is achieving its key control objectives and key business objectives for the areas reviewed.

For Sarbanes-Oxley Section 404 annual review of the bank account reconciliation, a traditional audit test with appropriate sampling techniques and probably attribute testing would need to be designed and performed. This testing for the annual Section 404 evaluation would probably take place once at an interim date. Based on the relative risk of bank account balances, and whether bank accounts would be considered a significant account under the PCAOB's criteria, bank accounts might also need to be tested around year-end. Since these Section 404 evaluations would probably be more robust than the ongoing monthly key control testing, the key controls testing would probably not need to be performed for the months when Section 404 testing was performed. The robustness of the Section 404 evaluations would enable management to both ensure and give assurance that management is achieving its key control objectives and key business objectives for the areas reviewed.

The mapping exercise and development of testing procedures for both our ongoing key controls review and Section 404 review would probably be documented in a testing document (potentially a checklist) that has listed the:

- Key control.
- Minimum standard of control.
- Monthly ongoing testing procedures.
- Annual Sarbanes-Oxley Section 404 testing procedures.

This testing document would also have an appropriate tick mark legend that would facilitate the easy documentation of the result of the testing performed. The following is offered for illustrative purposes:

TICK MARK LEGEND: (You <u>must</u> use one of the following tick marks)

✔   The minimum standard of control was achieved.

E   The minimum standard of control was <u>not</u> achieved. A description of the control exception, a proposed resolution, a resolution time line, and an estimate of the financial impact were reported. If the financial impact was potentially significant, then an explanation was provided as to why we have concluded the financial statements are fairly stated in accordance with GAAP.

N/A   The key accounting control is not applicable to this period.

I want to caution the reader that if you have developed control matrixes, you will want to maintain them on an ongoing basis. This is because a key controls checklist can only document and prove — based on the testing performed — the effectiveness of key controls. A control matrix is still necessary to document and prove the adequacy of control design. Over time as processes change, one will need to update the control matrixes in order to ensure the adequacy of control design.

When Do We Have Enough Key Controls?

As discussed in the last chapter, key controls are not all of the controls that were identified, tested, and relied upon to achieve the control objectives. So, how do you know if you have enough key controls? After you have developed minimum standards for all of the key controls identified for a process, activity, or account, trace them back to the control objectives. If all of the control objectives are adequately satisfied, then you have enough key controls identified.

Why is it a Minimum Standard?

In a quality control process, you define quality review points (key controls). These are points within the process where you must insure the appropriate quality level is achieved. In order to do this, you must establish a quality standard to which the actual achieved level can be compared. This standard is the acceptable level based on an appropriate understanding of the parameters of the system, the goals of management, and the costs and benefits related to achieving a higher or lower standard. This quality standard must also be based on the required level of quality that must be achieved to ensure adequate quality is consistently produced.

In most processes, it is not a problem if a higher level of quality is achieved. It may waste resources, and inconsistent quality can damage customer satisfaction. However, from an internal control perspective, producing a higher level of quality than is required is not generally a problem. However, producing a lower level of quality than is required is unacceptable and the product must be reworked to ensure the minimum standard of quality is achieved. Therefore, from an internal control perspective, the minimum standard of control quality must be achieved — and it is the ongoing standard that must be established and tested against to ensure management's objectives are being achieved.

Minimum standards of control must be based on the *maximum* amount of *risk* of control failure that management is willing to accept for a key control. This is an important concept and another way to view how minimum standards of control should be established. Internal control is a process intended to reduce or mitigate to an acceptable level the inherent risks in business processes. Control activities are not intended to eliminate all of the inherent risks because this would be inefficient and too costly. Therefore, in any internal control process, management has determined and incorporated into the process design an acceptable risk of control failure based on an analysis of the cost versus the benefit of different levels of internal control. This acceptable level is the maximum amount of risk of control failure that management is willing to accept. To further mitigate the risk would, again, be inefficient and too costly. To accept a greater amount of risk would not give adequate assurance of control achievement. Minimum standards of control should be based on the maximum amount of risk of control failure that management determines to be acceptable for a given key control.

Frequency of Review

How often do we need to review a key control against its minimum standard of control? In our bank account reconciliation process, are we willing to only reconcile bank accounts yearly? That seems a little long, since there is a risk that errors will go undiscovered and uncorrected if there is a large volume of large dollar transactions going through the account on a daily basis. This is, of course, because there is a greater risk of large dollar errors occurring. Likewise, if the account is essentially dormant, and only two small dollar transactions process through the account each year, then a yearly reconciliation seems reasonable. Therefore, the risk of control failure for our bank account reconciliation process is in part based on:

- The dollar size and number of transactions.
- The account balance over time.
- The period of time our bank account agreement allows for us to request adjustments.

There is more risk of the occurrence of undiscovered financial misstatements, irregularities, and financial losses if there is a high volume of large dollar denominated transactions. There is less financial risk if there are very few small dollar denominated transactions flowing through the account. These factors or financial risks of account misstatement (control failure) determine how often it is reasonable for management to reconcile the bank account. The norm for bank accounts is to reconcile them each month when bank statements are received from the bank. This is because the norm is to maintain bank accounts that have a high volume of activity. However, if one had a bank account with almost no activity, then it would probably be appropriate to reconcile it infrequently.

The **frequency of review,** or how often a key control is verified against its established minimum standard of control, is therefore determined based on the maximum amount of risk of control failure that management is willing to accept. One will find that the normal frequencies of key control verification are monthly, quarterly, and yearly. However, some key controls are so significant that they should be reviewed and verified against their defined minimum standard of control daily. Each key control must be evaluated and a frequency of review defined based on the maximum amount of risk of control failure that management is willing to accept.

Key Controls Monthly Review Process

Although the frequency of review for key controls will generally be daily, monthly, quarterly, or yearly, the key controls for an area of responsibility should generally be reviewed and certified, as a whole, each month. If a checklist approach is used, then all of the area's key controls along with a minimum standard of control per key control should be listed. The entire checklist of key controls would then be reviewed each month; however, only the key controls that were due to be reviewed for the current period would be reviewed. Of course, during the current period, and every period, all key controls with a daily or monthly frequency of review would be reviewed. Additionally, any quarterly or yearly key controls that were due to be reviewed would be reviewed. It should be noted that quarterly key controls could be reviewed on any month during a quarter, not just on a quarter end — just as yearly key controls can be due to be reviewed during any month of the year. Therefore, the yearly key control frequency is on a fiscal, not a year-end, basis. To ensure an appropriate key controls monthly review process, one must review each key control due to be reviewed for the current period against its established minimum standard of control.

Other Benefits of the Minimum Standard of Control

Once you have defined key controls and minimum standards of control for an activity, process, cycle, or account, you will find that key controls make an excellent training tool. For example, let us assume that you have just hired a new accountant who will be responsible for preparing bank account reconciliations. If you hand this person a listing of the accounts to reconcile and a well-defined listing of key controls, each with an equally well-defined minimum standard of control and frequency of review for the appropriate completion of bank account reconciliations, haven't you eliminated much of the misunderstanding that could occur if you had just handed them a list of bank accounts to reconcile?

Reviewing Key Controls and Control Exceptions

Based on the defined frequency of review, each key control must be evaluated against its defined minimum standard of control. If the minimum standard of control for a specific key control is not achieved, then this must be reported as a **"control exception."** The key controls process is predicated on the concept that for a given process, activity, or account balance, specific tasks must be completed correctly in order to achieve specific quality standards. Therefore, if the minimum standard of control is not achieved for a key control, then one of the right things is not getting done right.

Failure to achieve the minimum standard of control for a defined key control will happen. However, in theory it should not. This is because achieving the key control's minimum standard is something that needs to get done, and get done right. If this required task is not achieved to the required minimum level of established quality, management needs to know this control exception exists so that any risk can be appropriately mitigated.

In the next chapter we discuss how key controls should be reviewed and control exceptions should be identified, mitigated, and reported.

CHAPTER 6
THE KEY CONTROLS VERIFICATION AND EXCEPTION REPORTING PROCESS

> **"Controls don't slow you down; they allow you to go faster."**
> **— Tony Thompson**

Key Controls — Normal Monthly Validation, Review, and Reporting Process

During the normal monthly key control validation and review process, the following steps occur:

1. All personnel perform their normal monthly duties.

2. In order to meet established reporting due dates, all personnel (with assigned key control responsibilities) will review the key controls for which they are responsible against the established minimum standards of control based on the established frequencies of review.

3. All personnel will forward completed monthly key controls checklists to their supervisors for review. For any exception to achieve the established minimum standard of control for a key control, an appropriate mitigation plan must be submitted.

4. First-line supervisors/managers will complete the key controls checklists for their areas of responsibility. For many areas of responsibility, this will include summarizing the results of key control reviews performed by several areas, which report to the first-line supervisor/manager, to develop an overall result for the first-line supervisor's/manager's area of responsibility.

5. First-line supervisors/managers will next complete appropriate key control certifications for their areas of responsibility. First-line supervisors/managers will then review the significant events and judgments made within their areas of responsibility and complete this portion of the monthly certification for their areas of responsibility. The first-line supervisor/manager will then forward a signed combined key controls and significant events and judgments certification report to his or her immediate supervisor. All key control exceptions must be reported by the first-line supervisor/manager to the next level of management.

6. Senior managers will receive and review all key control certifications from the first-line supervisors/managers that report to them. Additionally, senior managers will review the significant events and judgments reported. Senior managers will summarize the results received from their direct reports and complete a summary key controls and significant events and judgments certification for their areas of responsibility. All key control exceptions must be reported by the senior manager to the next level of management.

7. Step 6 will be repeated for each additional level of management:

    • Most senior levels of management would report all key control exceptions. However, these exceptions should be categorized and prioritized from most significant to least significant.

    • All key control exceptions should be reported first to senior-level functional or operational management responsible for an area and then to the controller responsible for the area. The controller and management responsible for a registrant would then determine, based on the exceptions reported, the effectiveness of the registrant's internal control. When applicable, individual registrant management and the controller would then report on the registrant's internal control effectiveness so that an overall company opinion could be determined.

        a. As early as possible, registrant accounting management should discuss all reported significant internal control deficiencies with the company's external auditors to agree on the categorization and materiality of the issues.

    • A senior level of management may use appropriate materiality to exclude and not report immaterial key control exceptions, but this should, at least at first, only be controller level personnel who have an appropriate understanding of materiality and internal control deficiencies.

    • Registrant internal control effectiveness opinions and all significant key control exceptions should flow up to the audit committee and board of directors as appropriate to ensure adequate internal control issue visibility and resource allocation for timely resolution.

        a. Significant deficiencies and material weakness must be reported under Sarbanes-Oxley Act Section 302 to both the external auditor and the audit committee of the board of directors.

In this chapter, we discuss the monthly key controls verification and exception reporting processes. In Chapter 7, we discuss the significant events and judgments reporting process. And, in Chapter 8, we discuss the combined certification process to be utilized for both the key controls and significant events and judgments reporting processes.

Key Controls — Quality of the Review Process

To appropriately verify the *complete, accurate,* and *timely* achievement of a key accounting control, there must be:

- A person responsible for performing the key accounting control verification against the established minimum standard of control, and a different person who reviews and verifies that there was adequate **"evidence of control."**

- To have adequate *evidence of control*, sufficient evidence of the control's appropriate functioning must be:
    - Developed,
    - Reviewed,
    - Approved, and
    - Maintained as per the company's records retention policy.

It is the responsibility of the first-line supervisor or manager to review the evidence of control. The first-line supervisor/manager is defined as the first level of management in the organizational structure. Since the first line of management is responsible for and performs the evidence of control review, all higher levels of management are able to rely upon this review. However, appropriate supervision should ensure, at all levels of management, that the evidence of control reviews achieve established standards. Additionally, it is prudent to require each function/business unit head to ensure that all key controls for his or her areas of responsibility were reviewed for the period. This should generally be achieved via positive confirmation of the completion of all key controls reviews.

Key Control Testing and Sarbanes-Oxley Requirement Achievement

Based on Sarbanes-Oxley Act Section 302 requirements, management must review their disclosure controls and procedures and disclose their determination as to the effectiveness of these controls on a quarterly basis. Based on Sarbanes-Oxley Act Section 404 requirements, management must review their internal control over financial reporting and report on the effectiveness of these controls annually (as of each fiscal year-end). As mentioned in Chapter 2, one would test internal control over financial reporting at different times during the year to:

- Ensure the adequacy of control design.
- Ensure the effectiveness of control operation.
- Ensure company management to determine their assertion as to the effectiveness of internal control over financial reporting.
- Enable the company's external auditor to determine their audit opinion.

For the most part, internal control over financial reporting is a subset of the registrant's disclosure controls and procedures. Therefore, on an ongoing quarterly basis, one must review the registrant's disclosure controls and procedures in order to determine and support the required Section 302 evaluations and disclosures. Moreover, a key controls process is the best method to achieve compliance with these requirements. On an ongoing basis the key controls are evaluated against the determined minimum standards of controls based on the defined frequencies of review — none of which changes based on the Sarbanes-Oxley Act requirements for which compliance is being achieved.

However, what does change — significantly — is how the key control's achievement of the minimum standard is tested. For a monthly key controls review of account reconciliations, management may only review a listing of account reconciliations to ensure that all have been completed timely. This may be sufficient evidence and testing to achieve management's own monthly assurance requirements. On a quarterly basis this same level of testing may also be sufficient to support management's opinion on disclosure controls and procedures. However, on an annual basis to support an external audit of internal control over financial reporting, management may need to select a statistically valid sample of account reconciliations and perform attribute testing in order to ensure adequate review.

The annual audit of internal control over financial reporting will have the most stringent testing requirements. Quarterly and monthly testing of key controls should be integrated into an overall annual test plan to ensure that management's monthly assurance requirements, Section 302 quarterly requirements, and Section 404 annual requirements are all achieved. Company management should coordinate with their external auditor to ensure that he or she will be able to rely upon these test plans to reduce, to the greatest extent possible, the auditor's testing and that these test plans will be sufficient to support all of the required quarterly and annual evaluations, assertions, and disclosures.

Key Control Exceptions

In theory, there should be no exceptions to the achievement of a key control's established minimum standard of control. This is because the minimum standard was established as the minimum level of acceptable quality that must be achieved. Staffing levels and other resources should be provided to an area so that the management of that area is able to ensure all minimum standards are achieved. However, in reality, exceptions do occur. This is due to staffing changes, resource availability issues, and other control environment changes that effect management's ability to achieve the current level of work at the required minimum level of quality. When control exceptions occur, it is critical that management ensure that there is appropriate mitigation of the key control exceptions. For all exceptions to achieve the minimum standard of control established, the responsible manager/ supervisor must ensure that the following is provided and submitted:

- A description of the control exception
- A proposed resolution

- A proposed resolution estimated time line
- An estimate of the financial impact resulting from the exception

If the financial impact resulting from the exception is potentially significant, then an explanation must be provided as to why the submitting organization is able to conclude that its financial statements are stated in accordance with generally accepted accounting principles (GAAP).

Types of Key Control Exceptions

A review of some specific key control exceptions should enable you to understand both how to ensure appropriate reporting of these exceptions and why it is important. Therefore, we will review the following example key control exceptions:

- Automated process not working
- Inadequate segregation of duties
- Loss contingency

Automated Process Not Working

Let us assume that you receive a key control exception report and it states:

> A control weakness exists to the extent that a complete and accurate reconciliation of volumes and revenues is not possible between the old ABC and the new XYZ systems.

Now, in all cases, our key controls process should validate and strengthen our overall internal control structure. A key controls process should prove that the "right things" are getting done "right." However, the employee reporting this key control exception has not achieved this. In fact, instead of strengthening our overall internal control structure, the employee has created a question as to its adequacy. The question is whether the key control exception being reported is an inconsequential deficiency, a significant deficiency, or a material weakness? As you will recall from Chapter 2, according to the PCAOB's proposed accounting standard:

> A significant deficiency is an internal control deficiency that adversely affects the company's ability to initiate, record, process, or report external financial data reliably in accordance with generally accepted accounting principles. A significant deficiency could be a single deficiency, or a combination of deficiencies, that results in more than a remote likelihood that a misstatement of the annual or interim financial statements that is more than inconsequential in amount will not be prevented or detected.

> A material weakness is a significant deficiency that, by itself, or in combination with other significant deficiencies, results in more than a remote likelihood that a material misstatement of the annual or interim financial statements will not be prevented or detected.

The reporting of either a significant deficiency or a material weakness is always inappropriate within a key controls process. This is because the intent of a key controls process is to prevent these types of internal control weaknesses. The management of the area that reported this key control exception is responsible for ensuring that any key control exceptions are appropriately mitigated as fully explained earlier in this chapter. What has probably occurred is that the employee reporting this key control exception is either unaware of the responsibility to ensure appropriate mitigation steps are both taken and reported, or if appropriate mitigation occurred, then the employee simply does not know how to appropriately report the exception. The latter is usually what has occurred. Therefore, to ensure that the key control exception does not appear in our report to potentially be a significant deficiency or a material weakness, the following should be added:

> We have implemented appropriate manual procedures, which will ensure these systems are completely, accurately, and timely reconciled until the automated process issues are resolved.

This additional information should comply with the key control exception reporting requirements stated above and repeated here, that the following must be provided:

- A description of the control exception
- A proposed resolution
- A proposed resolution estimated time line
- An estimate of the financial impact resulting from the exception

One should note that the last bullet's requirements do not appear to be adequately satisfied by this additional statement. If the financial impact resulting from the exception is potentially significant, then an explanation must be provided as to why the submitting organization is able to conclude that its financial statements are stated in accordance with generally accepted accounting principles (GAAP). Therefore, to fully comply with this reporting requirement and to actually report a fully mitigated exception to achieve the minimum standard of control for a key control, the following should also be reported:

> We believe that the implemented manual processes adequately mitigate any risk and that the financial balances are fairly presented in all material respects.

With the addition of these two statements, the employee is able to show that the exception to achieve the key control's minimum standard of control was appropriately mitigated and that the financial statements are fairly stated. This is how key control exceptions should always be mitigated and reported.

The risk associated with not reporting key control exceptions correctly is better understood when one considers that management should share the results of the monthly key controls reviews with the company's internal and external auditors each month. Additionally, all key controls review documentation is potentially discoverable and could be subpoenaed, and as stated earlier — a key controls process should always validate and strengthen the overall internal control structure.

Inadequate Segregation of Duties

Let us assume in this case that you receive a key control exception report and it states:

> We have an inadequate segregation of duties within our ABC process.

Again the person reporting this key control exception has not done an appropriate job of reporting the required mitigation. Therefore, to report appropriate mitigation, the following should be added:

> We plan to increase staffing to resolve this situation next month. We have implemented additional manual review procedures, which internal audit has reviewed and approved.

In the above, the reporter of this exception has now proven that they did the "right thing," just as in the previous example. They implemented appropriate manual procedures to mitigate the risk caused by the key control exception. For any key control exception, management is always required to implement additional control procedures that will ensure adequate mitigation is achieved.

The following should also be added to demonstrate that the control failure risk caused by this key control exception is believed by management to be adequately mitigated:

> We believe these additional procedures adequately mitigate any risk.

Loss Contingency

Is there a problem if the following is reported as one of the monthly key accounting control exceptions?

> The total accounts receivable balance for XYZ Company is 8.5 million, with approximately 2.5 million currently over 120 days old. We estimate that it is probable that 1.5 million is uncollectible.

The first question you should ask yourself is, what is the materiality level for our financial audit. This is because, if this item were to be reported in a key controls certification at your company's fiscal year-end, you could have just reported a material weakness. As you will recall from Chapter 2, a material misstatement detected by the auditor's procedures that was not identified by the entity's management is indicative of a material weakness in internal control. If this were to occur, it would now be management's task to justify sufficiently to the external auditor why such an occurrence should not be considered a material weakness.

The problem with the exception as reported above is that the employee making the report did not have an adequate understanding of Statement of Financial Accounting Standards (FAS) No. 5, *Accounting for Contingencies*. The manner in which the exception is worded above would say, per the requirements of FAS No. 5, that the company should have recorded a loss contingency for the 1.5 million in accounts receivable.

Per FAS No. 5, *Accounting for Contingencies*, as a general rule:

> An estimated loss from a loss contingency (contingent liability) shall be accrued by a charge to income if *both* of the following conditions are met:
>
> 1. Information available prior to the issuance of the financial statements indicates that it is **probable** that an asset had been impaired or a liability had been incurred at the date of the financial statements.
>
> 2. The amount of the loss can be **reasonably estimated**.[1]

In the key control exception reported above, it was reported that "it is probable that 1.5 million is uncollectible." Because the loss was reported as being probable and a reasonable estimate was also reported, under FAS No. 5's requirements an appropriate contingent liability should have been accrued. There are more specific GAAP requirements for the appropriate accounting for accounts receivable than FAS No. 5. However, we specifically use an accounts receivable example to show the general usage to which FAS No. 5 can be applied as a guide.

In the example above, application of FAS No. 5 would mean that the accounts receivable should have been written off against the provision for bad debt. Therefore, to ensure that the accrual of appropriate contingent liabilities is not missed, or misreported, management should be adequately familiar with the requirements of FAS No. 5. Additionally, management should understand the importance of properly defining contingencies as "possible" rather than "probable," and loss estimates as being within a range of possibilities when appropriate.

Categorization and Prioritization of Key Control Exceptions

All key control exceptions must be categorized and prioritized. Within each category of key control exceptions reported, one should prioritize the issues so that the most significant issue is first and the least significant issue is last. This is, of course, to assist senior management in their review. Senior management only needs to be aware of key control exceptions that are not fully

---

[1]Paragraph 8 of FASB Statement No. 5, *Accounting for Contingencies*, copyrighted by the Financial Accounting Standards Board, 401 Merritt 7, P.O. Box 5116, Norwalk, Connecticut 06856, U.S.A., is reprinted with permission. Complete copies of this document are available from the FASB.

mitigated and have more than an inconsequential impact on the company's financial results. However, all key control exceptions should be reported to senior management so that they can ensure on an ongoing basis that all key control exceptions are being correctly categorized and prioritized. Also, all key control exceptions should be reviewed for cumulative effect, as will be explained shortly.

Step One: Categorization Based on Mitigation

From a key controls exception reporting perspective, all exceptions should first be categorized as either fully mitigated or not. Fully mitigated key control exceptions have:

- A proposed resolution, which shows that adequate mitigating controls are in place to ensure that management's control objectives are being adequately achieved.
- A proposed resolution estimated time line, which shows that management has taken appropriate steps to resolve the key controls exception on a timely basis.
- An estimate of the financial impact resulting from the exception, which clearly shows that any potential impact would be inconsequential to the fair presentation of the registrant's results of operations.

Step Two: Categorization of Non Fully Mitigated Exceptions

Next, one should categorize key control exceptions that are not fully mitigated. Such exceptions range from material to significant to inconsequential based on their potential impact on the registrant's ability to present fairly in all material respects their financial position and results of operations. Key control exceptions that are not fully mitigated and have a potential financial impact that is not considered to be inconsequential should be immediately reported to senior accounting management for their consideration. Senior accounting management would then determine the severity of these key control exceptions and whether these deficiencies are inconsequential, or can be resolved to become inconsequential. Appropriate materiality would need to be used to determine if these key control exceptions are significant deficiencies or material weaknesses. Accounting management should confirm their categorization of all potential significant deficiencies and material weaknesses with their external auditor. Confirmed significant deficiencies and material weaknesses would need to be formally reported to the audit committee of the board of directors as well as to the external auditor in order to comply with Sarbanes-Oxley Act Section 302 requirements.

Working Materiality Levels

In determining the severity of key control exceptions, one must use materiality. Of course, materiality is based on both qualitative and quantitative considerations, and it is inappropriate to develop or use a materiality standard for one's company that is based solely on a numerical threshold as explained in the Commission staff's *Staff Accounting Bulletin No. 99*. As already mentioned in Chapter 2, the PCAOB, in their proposed auditing standard, listed several internal control deficiencies that irregardless of potential financial statement impact should be considered at least significant deficiencies and potentially could be material weaknesses. However, in order to categorize and prioritize identified key control exceptions, materiality levels that are based on specific potential amounts of financial statement misstatement are very useful. I like to term these numerical thresholds as working materiality levels.

Of course, these working materiality levels should be conservative as they are used to identify key control exceptions that could potentially be severe enough to be considered significant deficiencies or material weaknesses, and management would not want to exclude from their consideration any key control exceptions that could potentially be significant. These working materiality levels should be developed and used for each registrant, as the materiality of potential financial statement misstatement is specific to each registrant. Management should also only use such devices as working materiality levels to assist them in the initial categorization and prioritization of key control exceptions that are not fully mitigated, provided that both qualitative and quantitative considerations are applied in making all final materiality judgments.

Section 404 Materiality Estimation

In order for management to be able to support an assertion that their internal control over financial reporting is effective, they must have both an adequate process and adequate evidential matter to enable them to prove:

- Sufficient procedures were applied to test both the adequacy of control design and the effectiveness of control operation.
- Such procedures must be supported by sufficient evidential matter, including documentation of both the design of internal control over financial reporting and the testing of the effective operation of such controls.
- Such evidential matter must provide reasonable support that:
    - Controls are adequately designed to prevent or timely detect material misstatements or omissions.
    - Tests were appropriately planned and executed.
    - The results of such tests were appropriately considered.

There probably are additional criteria that must be satisfied to prove an adequate process. However, no matter how adequate the process, it will be deemed to have been inadequate if it was ineffective. And, to be ineffective, only one material weakness needs to exist. One of the most important, if not the most important abilities in proving the effectiveness of internal control over financial reporting, is the ability to prove that the results were appropriately considered. The most important results that must be considered are the internal control deficiencies that were identified by both management and the external auditor in their reviews.

The possibility of a material misstatement's occurrence that would not be prevented or detected timely is all that is necessary to have a material weakness in internal control over financial reporting. No material misstatement must have occurred. A series or trend of significant deficiencies could be adequate evidence that a material weakness in internal control over financial reporting could occur that would not be prevented or detected timely. Therefore, the ability to analyze internal control deficiencies is critical to management's ability to evaluate the effectiveness of internal control over financial reporting.

One can only prove that their internal control over financial reporting is effective if they have the ability to identify and have identified all significant internal control deficiencies and have estimated the materiality of each singularly and in combination in order to prove for each SEC registrant that no material weaknesses exist.

One should recognize that only some of the key control exceptions would have a potential effect on the financial statements. However, the potential effect of all key control exceptions on the financial statements should be evaluated. In determining the materiality of key control exceptions, such should be considered both individually and in the aggregate for each SEC registrant to which the key control exceptions are applicable. This is due to the fact that several inconsequential exceptions can become consequential or even significant and several significant exceptions can become material. Therefore, it is critical to the determination of the effectiveness of a registrant's internal control over financial reporting that the "cumulative effect" of all internal control deficiencies/key control exceptions be considered.

Working materiality levels as described above should be developed to enable the efficient and effective estimation of the materiality of each internal control deficiency/key control exception. The materiality of each internal control deficiency/key control exception must be estimated individually; and then, for cumulative effect on each of the company's SEC registrants.

These working materiality levels should agree as much as possible with the levels utilized by the external auditor. Of course, all preliminary determinations made on this quantitative basis must be evaluated on a qualitative basis before final determinations are reached. The assistance of the external auditor in the development of the working materiality levels and the evaluation of internal control deficiencies would be most helpful.

The Reporting of Missing Key Controls

If a necessary key control has never been put in place, when identified as missing, it should be reported as a key control exception. The missing key control should continue to be reported until the control is put in place and validated to be working as designed.

Positive Confirmation of Key Control Exception Resolution

I recommend that key control exceptions be reported in the month that they are finally resolved. These exceptions should be reported as having been resolved to provide positive confirmation that the key control exception has been resolved. The alternative is that the key control exception will simply disappear from the certification report with only negative assurance that it was actually resolved and not just forgotten or missed.

Chapter Summary

It is important to understand that in a key controls process, failure to achieve the minimum standard of control established for a key control should always be avoided. However, when an exception to achieve the minimum standard of control occurs, management must take all necessary and appropriate steps to mitigate any associated risk. It is never appropriate to report a weakness in internal control. Instead, what should be reported is a key control exception whose risk to the internal control system has been fully mitigated.

CHAPTER 7
THE SIGNIFICANT EVENTS AND JUDGMENTS REPORTING PROCESS

"Risks not communicated are risks personally assumed."
— Biggs C. Porter

The Significant Events and Judgments Reporting Process

Key controls are static for a given process at any point in time, although they change over time. Management needs to be constantly surveying the control environment and identifying changes that will or have occurred so that they can assess the risks related to these events and judgments and prepare for them. To be able to prepare, there must be:

- An ongoing process to ensure appropriate control environment monitoring.
- A process that will facilitate the gathering of the information needed to alert management to these changes.
- A vehicle for the communication of these changes.

For each item communicated, management must assess its risk and ensure that appropriate action is determined and taken. The achievement of these objectives is the intent of the significant events and judgments reporting process.

Key Controls Versus Significant Events and Judgments Process

The key controls process is an ongoing quality control self-audit of internal control over existing business processes, while the significant events and judgments process is a review of the changes in the control environment in which the existing business processes exist and operate.

The significant events and judgments reporting process is based on a different theoretical approach than that of the key controls process.

Key Controls Theoretical Approach

The key controls process is based on the theory that key controls must be reviewed based on their established frequency of review against the established minimum standards of control. This self-audit approach, on an ongoing basis, ensures the quality control of internal control over existing business processes and both ensures and gives assurance that management is able to achieve their key business objectives.

All exceptions to achieve an established minimum standard for a key control must be reported. Key control exceptions must flow upward through the chain of command to senior management. At some level of management, appropriate materiality levels may be applied to assume the responsibility for resolving inconsequential key control exceptions. However, all significant and material exceptions must flow up to executive management and the audit committee and to the board of directors, as appropriate.

Significant Events and Judgments Process Theoretical Approach

The significant events and judgments process is based on a different theory. An employee may assume the risk of not communicating a control environment risk at any level in the corporation. However, a risk not communicated is a risk personally assumed. This means that one should not fail to communicate a control environment risk unless they are *certain* that they can appropriately handle this risk for the organization. The significant events and judgments reporting process is predicated upon the concept that an employee should report via the process those control environment risks that their boss should know about. Inherent in this is a concept that one should report certain items from the perspective that their boss should know about them even if the employee is fully capable of handling the risk. Communicating significant risks timely to one's boss — even risks that the employee intends to fully handle — is advised.

Significant Events and Judgments to Report

As was already mentioned, all employees should be surveying the control environment on an ongoing basis so that they can identify risks. The types of risks that need to be identified fall into two broad categories:

- Significant events
- Significant judgments

Significant Events

Significant events are just that, any significant event that has occurred or will occur that will effect the current control environment. From an accounting and financial reporting perspective, some examples include:

- Anticipated adoption of new or significant changes in existing accounting principles or methods.
- Anticipated new or changes in existing laws or regulations applicable to the company.

- Anticipated significant changes in existing accounting or financial reporting automated systems or the development of new systems.
- Anticipated significant changes that could result in required financial disclosures.
- Any significant accounting transaction that occurred or may occur.

Significant Judgments

Significant judgments those that an employee or lower level of management has made of which the "boss" or higher level of management should be aware. From an accounting and financial reporting perspective, examples include:

- Any significant accounting judgments or estimates recorded for the period or significant changes in existing accounting judgments and estimates.
- Any other significant judgments made to non-accounting estimates for the period of which higher-level management should be made aware.
- Any significant internal control concern not reported via the key controls reporting process, since it was not related to a key controls exception.

Of course, there are a multitude of different significant judgments that are made in a company on a monthly basis. These significant judgments may be related to the regulatory, finance, environmental, or other areas within the company. The types of significant judgments vary based on the area of the company; however, the requirement to report all significant judgments that one's boss should know about is a constant.

Timing of Reporting

Significant events and judgments are discussed and reported informally within companies on an ongoing basis and the implementation of this formal reporting process is not intended to affect this normal ongoing process. Instead, it is intended to strengthen it. This is achieved in two ways. The requirement to report these items each month for the prior period:

1. Reinforces the need for management to stay constantly vigilant to environmental risks.
2. Gives greater assurance that the control environment risks inherent in the reported significant events and judgments will be appropriately mitigated.

Significant Events and Judgments Reporting Examples

A review of how an example significant judgment should be reported will help you to understand both how to ensure appropriate reporting of these items and why it is important. Let us assume that the following significant judgment was reported:

Significant judgment was applied in making the mark to market revaluation of the XYZ contract.

Using significant judgment is something that must be done in making accounting estimates. However, in all cases, appropriate accounting estimates should be based on the best information available and this should be stated. In the above example, this was not stated and the reporting that significant judgment was applied in an accounting area does not in itself validate and strengthen our overall internal control environment. Therefore, to ensure that we are achieving this objective, the following should be added to the above:

Current accounting estimates were reviewed based on appropriate valuation and recognition principles and reserves were appropriately adjusted based on the best information available.

Management does not want a problem reported — they want a solution. Therefore, one must always address the potential exposure and needed mitigation directly when reporting a significant judgment. To do this, in this case, the following should also be added:

We believe the current estimates are appropriate and are fairly stated in all material respects.

Just as in the reporting of key control exceptions, in the reporting of significant events and judgments, the manager who reports them must take all necessary and appropriate steps to mitigate any risks. It is never appropriate to report a risk that is not adequately mitigated, if the manager reporting the risk is responsible for ensuring its appropriate mitigation. Therefore, when the reporting manager is responsible for the risk mitigation, he or she should always add an appropriate summation, as above, for higher-level management to let them know that any risk was appropriately mitigated

CHAPTER 8
THE KEY CONTROLS AND SIGNIFICANT EVENTS AND JUDGMENTS CERTIFICATION PROCESS

> **"You see things as they are and ask, 'Why?'**
> **I dream things as they never were and ask, 'Why not?'"**
> **— George Bernard Shaw**

Types of Certification Reports

There are generally three types of key controls certification reports. They differ due to the different responsibilities of the parties who complete them. The first-line supervisor/manager has different responsibilities than the senior manager. Additionally, function heads may use appropriate materiality levels when reporting to executive management.

For key controls exception reporting, all key control exceptions must be reported to a level of management that can ensure the issues are timely resolved. If a level of management is able to ensure the timely resolution of a key control exception and can be adequately relied upon to ensure this occurs, then that level of management can assume this responsibility. Obviously, only the most senior levels of function and business unit management should assume this responsibility. All lower levels should be required to report *all* key control exceptions through the chain of command until reaching this level of senior management. Additionally, this senior level will only *not* report inconsequential key control exceptions that they have assumed the responsibility for resolving. This senior level of management must understand internal control deficiencies and materiality in order to be able to assume the responsibility for resolving key control exceptions, and all significant and *material* key control exceptions *must* be reported to executive management, the audit committee, and board of directors as appropriate to ensure adequate visibility, resource allocation, and timely resolution.

First-line Supervisor's/Manager's Key Controls Certification Report

As mentioned earlier, the first-line supervisor/manager is responsible for ensuring that there was adequate evidence of control. Therefore, they should attest to this in their certifications. The following is an example of the types of representations that the first-line supervisor's/manager's certification should include:

1. I have reviewed the evidence of control for the key controls for which I am responsible against the specific standard of control for each key control.
2. Such review was completed in compliance with the key controls test plans established for my areas of responsibility for the period reviewed.
3. Based on this review and in accordance with appropriate governance policy, *all exceptions* to the achievement of the specific minimum standards of control are reported.
4. Additionally, I certify that all of the evidence of control that I reviewed was:
    i. Complete and accurate.
    ii. Appropriately reviewed and approved.
    iii. Sufficient evidence upon which to base and support the above and following assertions.

(The "following assertions" will be discussed after the next section.)

Appropriate review and approval of the evidence of control by the first-line supervisor/manager is critical to the success of a key controls process. Management at every level of the company, including the board of directors, relies upon this review. Across departments, company management should strive to achieve a consistent level of quality for these reviews of the evidence of control. This does not mean all departments must use the same control processes. Based on differences in staffing levels and other resources, this may not be possible or even desirable. However, what is required is that a consistent quality level is established and that everyone strives to achieve it.

Special Key Controls Verification Requirement

Many different employees in many different organizations across the company will be responsible for certifying that they have reviewed the key controls for their areas of responsibility and that the key controls' minimum standards were adequately achieved. A consistent level of review quality must be achieved in that management must always know that when no key control exceptions are reported, that in fact the key controls were reviewed and the established key control minimum standards of control were achieved. To ensure this, management must make it clear to all employees who complete key control reviews that the penalty for false reporting is immediate termination. This is not to suggest that mistakes will not be made. However, deliberate failure to verify correctly key controls within one's area of responsibility cannot be tolerated. This is, of course, because everyone within the organization is depending upon these key controls reviews occurring according to the standards established.

Assertions Required of All Reporting Levels

There are certain assertions that all levels of management who report on key controls and significant events and judgments should be required to make in each certification. For example, all levels of management should be responsible for the accounting transactions made within their areas of responsibility. Some levels of management, especially in the accounting areas are responsible for the accuracy of account balances. Higher levels of management in both accounting and business unit management are responsible for the fair presentation of financial statements. Therefore, all certifying managers are at a minimum responsible for the accounting transactions they generate within their areas of responsibility, and the following is intended to enable them to correctly attest to this for their areas of responsibility:

> On the basis of the key controls review performed, and taking into account the key control exceptions reported and significant accounting events and judgments noted, I certify that the financial transactions, account balances, and financial statements, if any, within my areas of responsibility are for the period presented fairly in all material respects.

There are three additional attestations that all managers should be required to make based on the need to support the principle executive and financial officers in their required Sarbanes-Oxley Act Section 302 certifications. These suggested assertions are:

1. I certify that the key controls review performed was adequate to ensure that all deficiencies in the design and/or operation of these internal controls, which could adversely affect our ability to record, process, summarize, and report financial data, were appropriately identified and disclosed.

2. I certify that any fraud, whether or not material, that involves management or other employees who have a significant role in internal control was disclosed, whether this fraud was discovered based on this review or became known to me otherwise during the period.

3. I certify that based on my future knowledge, I will inform my manager timely if there are any significant changes in internal controls, significant changes in Securities and Exchange Commission (SEC) required disclosures, or in other factors that could significantly affect internal controls subsequent to the date of this certification

Senior Manager's Certification Report

The only thing that makes a senior manager a senior manager for this reporting purpose is that he or she has a first-line supervisor/manager reporting to them who is responsible for evaluating and attesting to the evidence of control. If, however, this manager also has first-line responsibilities, then he or she is a first-line manager for this reporting purpose and should use the first-line manager's report format. If and only if a manager has no first-line responsibilities, then this manager is a senior manager for reporting purposes and should use the senior manager certification report format.

Obviously, the first difference in the senior manager's report format is that it will not have an attestation as to the quality of the evidence of control. However, all of the attestations enumerated above that are required of all certifying managers should be and are included in the senior manager's report.

For example purposes, I have included sample verbiage for a senior manager's monthly certification report:

I have, for **XYZ Department,** established appropriate policy and procedures to assure the company that an acceptable system of internal control will be maintained for my areas of responsibility. These measures were created to provide a process:

- To identify required key controls.
- To implement these key controls.
- To report *all* exceptions to the achievement of key controls' minimum standards.
- To ensure an ongoing risk assessment in order to timely identify and report significant events and judgments.

Additionally, I (and the personnel reporting to me) have reviewed our system of key controls. We have identified and implemented during the period any necessary enhancements to this system to ensure that it will continue to provide an adequate evaluation of the system of internal control, which will support the conclusions reached. Based on the enhancements identified and implemented, I (and the personnel reporting to me) certify that our key controls process is both appropriately adequate in design and effective in operation to support all of the standards established and the assertions and certifications made.

I have reviewed the results of our key controls review, the reported significant accounting events and judgments, and the results of any independent review of the accounting system carried out during the period to determine to my own satisfaction the achievement of our internal control objectives.

Based on this review, I certify to the best of my knowledge and belief that:

- On the basis of the key controls review performed, and taking into account the key control exceptions reported and significant accounting events and judgments noted, I certify that the financial transactions, account balances, and financial statements, if any, within my areas of responsibility are for the period presented fairly in all material respects.

- The key controls review performed was adequate to ensure that all deficiencies in the design and/or operation of these internal controls, which could adversely affect our ability to record, process, summarize, and report financial data, were appropriately identified and disclosed

- Any fraud, whether or not material, that involves management or other employees who have a significant role in internal control was disclosed, whether this fraud was discovered based on this review or became known to me otherwise during the period.

- Based on my future knowledge, I will inform my manager timely if there are any significant changes in internal controls, significant changes in SEC required disclosures, or in other factors that could significantly affect internal controls subsequent to the date of this certification

Function/Business Unit Head Certification Report

As discussed at the beginning of this chapter, at some level of senior management it may be appropriate to only report consequential key control exceptions. Therefore, the above senior manager's report would be updated to state that only significant and material exceptions to the achievement of key controls minimum standards were reported.

Again, only the most senior levels of function and business unit management should assume this responsibility, and only if they understand appropriately internal control deficiencies and materiality. All lower levels should be required to report *all* key control exceptions through the chain of command until reaching this level of senior management. Additionally, this senior level of management will only *not* report inconsequential key control exceptions that they have assumed the responsibility for resolving. All consequential key control exceptions must be reported to executive management, the audit committee, and board of directors as appropriate to ensure adequate visibility, resource allocation, and resolution.

Significant Events and Judgments Reporting

Because all levels within the company have the same requirements for reporting significant events and judgments, a single format is appropriate for all levels of management. If possible, the reporting of significant events and judgments should be integrated into the key controls monthly certification reports so that only one report is required.

CHAPTER 9
KEY CONTROLS AND COSO'S
INTERNAL CONTROL FRAMEWORK

> **"By constant self-discipline and self-control,
> you can develop greatness of character."**
> — Grenville Kleiser

Internal Control Framework Requirement

One of the requirements that must be achieved to be able to comply with Sarbanes-Oxley Act Section 404 is that public registrants must adopt and apply an authoritative framework for internal control. This is first an audit requirement. Your external auditor will need you to have adopted a framework for internal control so that there is a set of criteria against which your company's system of internal control can be compared. Without a framework, there would be no such criteria and your external auditor would be unable to determine how well you had achieved the criteria's objectives.

Second, the Securities and Exchange Commission (SEC), in their final rules on the Sarbanes-Oxley Act Section 404, required a company to include in their annual internal control report of management a statement identifying the framework used by management to conduct the required evaluation of the effectiveness of the company's internal control over financial reporting. The SEC's final rules require companies to adopt a suitable, recognized control framework that is established by a body or group that has followed due process procedures, which must include the broad distribution of the framework for public comment. Therefore, you will be required to adopt and disclose an authoritative framework. Here are a few examples of the many frameworks from which to choose:

- COSO – *Internal Control - Integrated Framework*
- CoCo – *The Control Model* (Canadian Institute of Chartered Accountants)
- *Turnbull Report – Internal Control: Guidance for Directors on the Combined Code* (Institute of Chartered Accountants in England and Wales)
- ACC – *Australian Criteria of Control* (The Institute of Internal Auditors - Australia)
- *The King Report* (The Code of Corporate Practices & Conduct from The Institute of Directors of Southern Africa)

Although within the United States the COSO framework is the best known and accepted, the SEC did not mandate its usage. Rather they stated:

> The COSO framework satisfies our criteria and may be used as an evaluation framework for purposes of management's annual internal control evaluation and disclosure requirements. However, the final rules do not mandate use of a particular framework, such as the COSO framework, in recognition of the fact that other evaluation standards exist outside of the United States, and that frameworks other than COSO may be developed within the United States in the future that satisfy the intent of the statute without diminishing the benefits to investors. The use of standard measures that are publicly available will enhance the quality of the internal control report and will promote comparability of the internal control reports of different companies. The final rules require management's report to identify the evaluation framework used by management to assess the effectiveness of the company's internal control over financial reporting.

> Specifically, a suitable framework must: be free from bias; permit reasonably consistent qualitative and quantitative measurements of a company's internal control; be sufficiently complete so that those relevant factors that would alter a conclusion about the effectiveness of a company's internal controls are not omitted; and be relevant to an evaluation of internal control over financial reporting.

CobiT for Information Systems

The mission of CobiT as per the Information Systems Audit and Control Association's (ISACA) Web site (www.isaca.org) is, "To research, develop, publicise, and promote an authoritative, up-to-date, international set of generally accepted IT Control Objectives for day-to-day use by business managers as well as security, control, and audit practitioners." Therefore, for an internal control framework with control objectives for information and related technology, you will probably want to use CobiT. The CobiT Executive Summary, is available on the ISACA's Web site.

FDICIA for the Banking Industry

Many companies (especially those in the banking industry) in the United States are subject to the requirements of the Federal Deposit Insurance Corporation Improvement Act (FDICIA). Under this legislation, companies with an asset size of $500 million must have already adopted an internal control framework, and it would appear that the framework adopted is generally COSO.

COSO Internal Control – Integrated Framework

The best-known authoritative framework for internal controls in the United States is *Internal Control - Integrated Framework,* which was developed by the Committee of Sponsoring Organizations of the Treadway Commission and is sponsored by the following organizations:

- AICPA – American Institute of Certified Public Accountants
- AAA – American Accounting Association
- FEI – Financial Executives International
- IIA – The Institute of Internal Auditors
- IMA – Institute of Management Accountants

This framework is generally referred to as the COSO framework. The framework was issued in a volume set and you can obtain copies from the American Institute of Certified Public Accountants (www.aicpa.org). The executive summary is published on the COSO Web site (www.coso.org). Due to the COSO framework's wide acceptance in the United States, this is probably the framework that your company should adopt for domestic operations; and, therefore, it is the only one I am going to describe in detail.

Foreign operations may, however, choose to adopt another framework, for example the *Turnbull Report*. Adopting the *Turnbull Report* as one's internal control framework may make sense if, for example, the foreign operations are in the United Kingdom. In this situation, the management and accountants of your foreign operations and the area's external auditors will probably be chartered accountants and therefore they would be certified by the Institute of Chartered Accountants in England and Wales. In this case, they will probably be most familiar with the *Turnbull Report* as an internal control framework rather than COSO since it was developed by the Committee on Corporate Governance of the Institute of Chartered Accountants in England and Wales, in conjunction with the London Stock Exchange. Since the predominant internal control framework adopted in their area is the *Turnbull Report* — and it meets the criteria set forth by the Commission as a suitable framework — why not allow the foreign operations to adopt it? There could be operational concerns related to ensuring an adequate understanding of accounting principles generally accepted in the United States (GAAP) and the COSO framework among the foreign operation's accounting management. However, if no concerns exist, and there is an acceptable regional internal control framework, then it would probably be more efficient and effective to allow the management of foreign operations to adopt the internal control framework that is predominant in their area of operations and is probably best known, understood, and accepted by both themselves and their external auditors. I would, however, suggest that the domestic corporate management obtain some comfort in relation to the foreign area's framework before allowing its adoption.

The rest of this chapter is an overview of the most important points to understand about the COSO framework. Then, we will explore how the key controls process integrates into this framework.

As you should remember from Chapter 1, COSO's definition of internal control is:

> Internal control is a process, affected by an entity's board of directors, management, and other personnel, designed to provide reasonable assurance regarding the achievement of objectives in the following categories:
>
> - Effectiveness and efficiency of operations.
> - Reliability of financial reporting.
> - Compliance with applicable laws and regulations.

The COSO Integrated Framework uses three theoretical dimensions to develop a framework and criteria for management to evaluate internal control.

A cube is generally used to represent these dimensions.

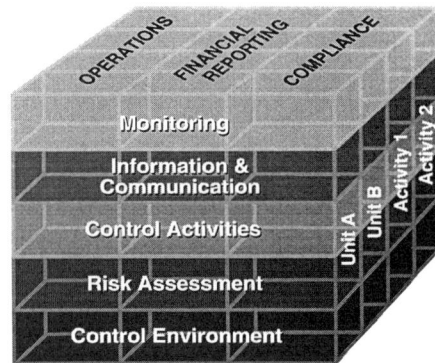

COSO Dimensions of Internal Control

The first dimension, which is listed across the top of the cube, is the control objective "categories." These are the same categories as listed in COSO's definition of internal control. One should note that these objective categories are essentially those of management's internal control objectives. According to the COSO framework, if one were to summarize all of the different types of control objectives that management has for all of the different types of business processes, one would be able to categorize any control objective at the highest level of summarization as belonging to one of these three categories. Therefore, according to the COSO framework, all of management's internal control efforts are intended to achieve adequate control that will ensure:

- Effective and efficient operations.
- Reliable financial reporting.
- Compliance with applicable laws and regulations.

The second dimension consists of five interrelated components of internal control. The five components are listed on the face of the cube:

- Monitoring
- Information and communication
- Control activities

- Risk assessment
- Control environment

All five components are applicable to each of the control objective categories, and each of the five components of internal control is required to be able to achieve the three objective categories. These five components are a summarization of the control processes that management uses to achieve objective categories. There is a direct relationship between the objective categories, which are what an entity strives to achieve, and the components of internal control, which represent the required elements of internal control that are necessary to be able to achieve the objective categories.

In the COSO framework, the cube represents the entire enterprise. The cube or enterprise is composed of business units, and then activities within the business units. The business units and activities are listed on the side of the cube and they represent the third dimension of internal control. The third dimension of internal control emphasizes that internal control is critical to the entire enterprise and to all of its components.

COSO Integrated Framework Internal Control Review

According to the COSO framework, the five components of internal control must be present and adequate at the activity or process level where transactions are processed and throughout the entire entity in order to enable management to be able to achieve its control objectives in the three objective categories. Therefore, to ensure compliance with the COSO framework, management should for each objective category:

1. Evaluate and assess each of the five components of internal control, and
2. These assessments should take place at the activity level, business unit level, and for the entire enterprise.

An internal control evaluation based on the criteria above can support a conclusion that internal control is effective for each of the three objective categories, if the board of directors and management have reasonable assurance that:

- They understand the extent to which the entity's effectiveness and efficiency of operations objectives are being achieved.
- Reliable published financial statements are being prepared.
- The company is adequately complying with applicable laws and regulations.

Sarbanes-Oxley Act Section 404 Internal Control Review

Based on Sarbanes-Oxley Act Section 404, management is only required to evaluate one of the COSO *Internal Control - Integrated Framework's* objective categories — the reliability of financial reporting. The SEC, in their final rules on Section 404, stated that:

> We recognize that our definition of the term "internal control over financial reporting" reflected in the final rules encompasses the subset of internal controls addressed in the COSO Report that pertains to financial reporting objectives. Our definition does not encompass the elements of the COSO Report definition that relate to effectiveness and efficiency of a company's operations and a company's compliance with applicable laws and regulations, with the exception of compliance with the applicable laws and regulations directly related to the preparation of financial statements, such as the Commission's financial reporting requirements.

To be able to perform a Section 404 evaluation and develop its assessment of the effectiveness of internal control over financial reporting, the SEC stated that:

> The assessment of a company's internal control over financial reporting must be based on procedures sufficient both to evaluate its design and to test its operating effectiveness. Controls subject to such assessment include, but are not limited to: controls over initiating, recording, processing, and reconciling account balances, classes of transactions and disclosure and related assertions included in the financial statements; controls related to the initiation and processing of non-routine and non-systematic transactions; controls related to the selection and application of appropriate accounting policies; and controls related to the prevention, identification, and detection of fraud. The nature of a company's testing activities will largely depend on the circumstances of the company and the significance of the control. However, inquiry alone generally will not provide an adequate basis for management's assessment.

> An assessment of the effectiveness of internal control over financial reporting must be supported by evidential matter, including documentation, regarding both the design of internal controls and the testing processes. This evidential matter should provide reasonable support: for the evaluation of whether the control is designed to prevent or detect material misstatements or omissions; for the conclusion that the tests were appropriately planned and performed; and that the results of the tests were appropriately considered. The public accounting firm that is required to attest to, and report on, management's assessment of the effectiveness of the company's internal control over financial reporting also will require that the company develop and maintain such evidential matter to support management's assessment.

COSO's Components of Internal Controls and Key Controls

Now that you have a basic understanding of the COSO integrated framework, our next task is to explain how a key controls process integrates into this framework. The best way to achieve this is to explain each of the COSO components of internal control and how a key controls process can assist you to evaluate these components.

Monitoring of Internal Control

Internal control systems need to be monitored because they change over time. When a company's processes change, the internal control system usually also needs to be changed. However, the company can fail to redesign internal controls as required. Company personnel can also fail to perform effectively designed controls. This is why a review of internal control is only valid for a point in time. One can only evaluate an internal control and determine if it was effectively designed and operated effectively as of the point in time for which it was reviewed. Therefore, systems of internal control must be monitored on an ongoing basis.

The key controls process is designed to ensure that business activities and processes are monitored on an ongoing basis. Each key control is assigned a frequency of review based on how often this individual key control needs to be monitored. The monthly key control process ensures that control weaknesses are timely identified and communicated to the appropriate level of management to ensure that any risks of control failure are appropriately mitigated. The key controls process is superior to any monitoring process that does not have established:

- Key controls (quality control monitoring points).
- Minimum standards (risk-based quality control review standards).
- Review frequencies (risk-based monitoring frequencies).
- Reporting requirements (risk-based mitigation standards).
- Certification requirements (standards for the overall quality required of the process).

The key controls process ensures that material exceptions are forwarded up through both the business unit and the functional chain of command, with serious matters reported to top management and the board of directors or its audit committee as appropriate.

The significant events and judgments process is also an ongoing monitoring activity. Although significant events and judgments are only summarized and reported monthly for the prior month's activity, the process causes management to remain vigilant and to ensure that the risk associated with significant events and judgments are appropriately mitigated and communicated. This significant events and judgments process does not replace the normal ongoing monitoring processes of management. Instead, it reinforces and monitors the process.

Information and Communication

Complete, accurate, and timely information is required at all levels within an organization to be able to operate the business and to ensure the achievement of the organization's objectives. In our modern business environment, information systems must generally capture and communicate all of the information necessary to enable informed business decision-making and reliable and compliant external reporting. In the COSO framework, "information systems" is conceptualized as a much broader concept, including both manual and computerized processes. It includes all processes necessary to ensure effective identification, capture, and communication of internal and external information. The objective of an organization's information systems is to ensure effective communication. Communication channels must exist that enable information to effectively and efficiently flow up, down, and across the organization. In addition, there must be adequate internal control over these information and communication channels.

Information is the lifeblood of a modern company, and it is the information systems that carry this blood throughout the organization. Key controls validate the information system's internal controls and ensure that the information produced is complete, accurate, reliable, and timely. Key controls also ensure that the security system is appropriate to ensure access to information assets is appropriately limited, access is appropriately based on one's assigned duties, and there is appropriate accountability for one's actions.

A key controls process helps employees to understand their very important role in ensuring the quality of the company's information gathering and processing activities. A key controls process also assists in ensuring the quality of the information communicated with external parties.

A significant events and judgments process assists management in the identification of environmental risks that can affect the quality of their information and communication channels, and ensures that there is a means of communicating significant information upstream.

Control Activities

Control activities are all of the methods employed by management to achieve control objectives. These include the policies and procedures management develops. Control activities occur throughout the organization and at all levels of the organization. Examples of control activities are approvals, verifications, reconciliations, and segregation of duties.

Key controls are, of course, a process designed to identify the key control activities within an organization and to ensure that these activities are achieving the control objectives of management.

Risk Assessment

The environments in which modern organizations operate are constantly changing. Although these organizations establish business objectives, the likelihood of internal changes and external environmental changes effecting the achievement of these objectives causes risk. All organizations, therefore, need a process by which they can effectively identify and communicate these risks to the appropriate levels of management who can ensure appropriate actions are taken.

For an existing business process, a key controls process ensures that the key controls within the process are determined and are evaluated timely against established standards. The key controls process assists management with risk assessment because it is a process that enables the monitoring of how the internal control system is achieving management's established control objectives and tracks and communicates how the risks are being mitigated.

The significant events and judgments process is used to monitor and report the special risks associated with change in the environment in which the existing business process operates. These changes can be both internal and external.

Additionally, in the next chapter on Enterprise Risk Assessment and Management, we will explain how a key controls process can become an even more integral and important part of the risk monitoring, assessment, and management process.

Control Environment

The control environment establishes and is the control culture of the company. It controls how employees feel about control. The control environment influences management style and philosophy within the organization in relation to integrity and ethical values. The control environment emanates from the board of directors downward, influencing all of the company's control processes and all of the other components of internal control.

It is probably obvious to anyone after reading the above how important the control environment is to the overall system of internal control. It is the control environment that is responsible for establishing and setting the "tone at the top." According to the COSO framework, the control environment encompasses factors listed below which are present in all companies:

- Integrity and ethical values
- Commitment to competence
- Board of directors or audit committee
- Management's philosophy and operating style
- Organizational structure
- Assignment of authority and responsibility

Each of these factors or attributes has "points of focus" that are high-level control objectives defined for these different areas. The points of focus are provided in the *Internal Control – Integrated Framework Evaluation Tools* book. These points of focus are an excellent source from which customized control objectives could be developed for many processes.

Control Environment Key Controls

The key controls process, once implemented and working as designed, becomes an integral and critical part of a company's control environment. To ensure the key controls process is adequately maintained over time, there are two control environment specific key controls that must be universally adopted:

1. Monthly review of the key controls, established minimum standards of control, and certification frequencies to ensure that all necessary and appropriate changes were made for any system or process changes that took place during the period.

2. On an annual or other reasonable basis, one must review all of the above and update the documentation that supports one's key controls process.

Additional control environment key controls may be necessary for specific control environment weaknesses. For example, if your company's control environment had a weakness in that you could not track when temporary employees left the company in order to ensure the timely termination of their access to your information systems, then one would probably need to develop an appropriate universal key control. This universal key control for security access review would probably require a monthly review to determine if a temporary person left your area of responsibility and then require a review of the security access for any temporary persons who had left.

Many control environment processes may be centrally owned within the enterprise and adequately maintained such that having key controls established at the enterprise level for this centralized function would be sufficient and prevent the need to review this area again at the activity level. For example, in an entity that has a compliance officer who is responsible for ensuring adherence to the code of conduct for the entire enterprise, all records of yearly sign-off on the code of conduct by employees, investigations, and other records would be centrally maintained. Key controls established to verify the achievement of control objectives for this centralized function would probably be sufficient. One would not need to have similar key controls for code of conduct review at the activity level. However, an area may or may not be adequately controlled at the enterprise level by a central function. Where the function is not adequately controlled at the enterprise level, the different responsible managers would need key controls.

For example, here is a partial listing of some control environment areas where one may want to have key controls established:

- Development and review of policies and procedures
- Update of process/activity desk procedures
- Update of employee job descriptions
- Completion of employee evaluations
- Achievement of business plan objectives (functional area)
- Achievement of employee training objectives
- Update/maintenance of business continuity plan

Again, these are just examples. However, all of these areas relate to the control environment and must be adequately controlled. If control is not ensured adequately by key controls at a centralized function, then additional key controls are necessary at the process owner level.

Control Environment Self-assessment Certifications

The preferred method of evaluating the control environment is to develop an adequacy of key controls. However, during the development process it may become necessary to supplement the key controls that review the control environment with self-assessment certifications. If this becomes necessary, then the self-assessment certifications could be based on the COSO control environment factors/attributes. Additionally, if the key controls process is originally implemented to only satisfy Sarbanes-Oxley Act Section 404 evaluation requirements, then one may be able to use self-assessment certifications to achieve adequate coverage of the two remaining COSO objective categories on an interim basis (operational efficiency and effectiveness and compliance with laws and regulations). The goal of the key controls program should be, however, to eventually have sufficient key controls in place across the enterprise to achieve an ongoing evaluation of all three COSO objective categories.

CHAPTER 10
KEY CONTROLS AND ENTERPRISE RISK ASSESSMENT AND MANAGEMENT

> **"Real knowledge is to know the extent of one's ignorance."**
> **— Confucius**

Enterprise Risk Assessment and Management

Let us assume that you have developed a key controls process that includes an integrated, ongoing risk assessment process similar to the significant events and judgments process described in Chapter 7. The next step then is to develop an ongoing process that will ensure the risks identified are appropriately managed. Since COSO has issued a risk management conceptual framework exposure draft, I only intend to give general direction as to how one would integrate a key controls process into an enterprise risk assessment and management process for maximum benefit.

The approach to accomplish this thus far has been based on the concept of embedding into the business much of what internal audit traditionally is responsible for accomplishing. The next step is to develop risk monitoring and management forums.

Risk Monitoring and Management Forum

A risk monitoring and management forum is a management team whose mission will be to review the overall risk assessment processes and reported issues for their areas of responsibility on a basis that will ensure that the COSO objective categories are adequately achieved. As a starting point, they will begin by reviewing the key controls processes.

Key Controls Process Review

To be able to sustain a key controls process on an ongoing basis, the management for each area must be responsible for maintaining the key controls process. The risk monitoring and management forum is a way to accomplish this goal and will be responsible for:

- Reviewing the monthly key controls certifications for their areas of responsibility and ensuring that key control exceptions are adequately mitigated or action plans are developed.

- Reviewing the actual key controls established for their areas of responsibility. This should be accomplished by scheduling reviews of the key controls for each area of responsibility based on a risk-based review schedule. An audit universe type approach to determining review frequencies could be used.

- Review of the significant events and judgments identified and reported monthly for their areas of responsibility. Please note that the significant events and judgments process should ensure adequate risk identification and reporting or risk assessment occurs; however, the risk monitoring and management forum is a vehicle to be used to ensure that the risks identified and reported are appropriately monitored and managed by a cross-functional management team.

- Ensuring that the internal control documentation that supports the key controls process is appropriately updated and maintained both for significant changes in internal control that occur during the period and on an annual basis in order to ensure such documentation is always current and sufficient.

- Ensuring that key control processes are timely developed for new areas.

- Review of the control environment for their areas of responsibility:

  - This would entail reviewing the code of conduct, delegation of authority, policies and procedures, and other practices in their areas of responsibility as explained in Chapter 9.

  - Review of and assessment of overall risks within their areas of responsibility. This should result in the development of a listing of the top tier risks for their areas of responsibility along with the development of action plans to ensure that appropriate steps are implemented on a reasonable time frame to address and mitigate these risks.

Quarterly, monthly, or even weekly meetings of the risk monitoring and management forum would be scheduled as appropriate. On a quarterly basis, the risk monitoring and management forum should be responsible for completing an overall risk-based control environment self-assessment. The result of this review should be a document in which the risk monitoring and management forum states:

- The areas reviewed and the review procedures utilized in the review.

- Risk-based control environment exposures along with action plans to mitigate these risks.

- Conclusions as to the adequacy of all components of internal control for their areas of responsibility on both an overall basis and a process-by-process basis as supported by the key controls certifications and other review processes and procedures applied.

- An overall conclusion as to the adequacy of the achievement of the COSO objective categories for their areas of responsibility.

The risk monitoring and management forums would then report to a higher-level committee on a monthly or quarterly basis. Depending on the size of the company, there could be several levels of higher committees. However, the highest committee should be a corporate committee that will then reach appropriate conclusions as to the adequacy of achievement of the COSO objective categories for the entire enterprise based on all of the overall risk-based control environment self-assessments received from the risk monitoring and management forums. This result would be communicated to the audit committee, and it would provide a basis for supporting the annual Sarbanes-Oxley Act Section 404 management assessment of internal control over financial reporting and the quarterly Sarbanes-Oxley Section 302 required review of the company's disclosure controls and procedures.

To be able to embed appropriately a non-biased risk monitoring and management process within the risk monitoring and management forums, the forums must be composed of a diverse set of cross-functional management who will ensure an independent challenge is performed and that there is adequate visibility of issues. The forums should also ensure that appropriate action plans are developed for identified issues. These action plans should include assigned responsibility and accountability for resolving the issues. Adequate visibility should include the ability to raise significant issues and risks to executive management and to the audit committee as appropriate to ensure adequate resources are made available for timely issue resolution.

Other Risk Areas

Different companies will have different areas of risk depending on their industries and the diversity of the products and services that they produce and provide. Depending on the specific needs of the company, there are several other areas of risk assessment and management that one may want to integrate into one or more of the company's risk monitoring and management forums. For example:

- Business plan risks
- Compliance risks
- Due diligence over projects and acquisitions
- Credit risk
- Insurable risks
- Other risks

CHAPTER 11
KEY CONTROLS AND DISCLOSURE CONTROLS AND PROCEDURES

> **"A pint of sweat saves a gallon of blood."**
> **— General George S. Patton**

Disclosure Controls and Procedures

On August 29, 2002, the Securities and Exchange Commission (SEC) published their final rules "Certification of Disclosure in Companies' Quarterly and Annual Reports" pursuant to the Sarbanes-Oxley Act Section 302 required certification of the principle executive and financial officers for certain SEC registrants. Within these new rules, the SEC promulgated a new term — **"disclosure controls and procedures."** We discussed this term in Chapter 2. However, in this chapter, we will go into much more detail. Therefore, according to the SEC's rules release:

> For purposes of the new rules, "disclosure controls and procedures" are defined as controls and other procedures of an issuer that are designed to ensure that information required to be disclosed by the issuer in the reports filed or submitted by it under the Exchange Act is recorded, processed, summarized, and reported, within the time periods specified in the Commission's rules and forms. "Disclosure controls and procedures" include, without limitation, controls and procedures designed to ensure that information required to be disclosed by an issuer in its Exchange Act reports is accumulated and communicated to the issuer's management, including its principal executive and financial officers, as appropriate to allow timely decisions regarding required disclosure.

The SEC further explained:

> We have defined the term "disclosure controls and procedures" to make it explicit that the controls contemplated by Section 302(a)(4) of the Act are intended to embody controls and procedures addressing the quality and timeliness of disclosure. We also have included this definition to differentiate this concept of disclosure controls and procedures from the preexisting concept of "internal controls" that pertains to an issuer's financial reporting and control of its assets, as currently embodied in Section 13(b) of the Exchange Act and as addressed in Sections 302(a)(5) and (a)(6) and Section 404 of the Act. We make this distinction based on our review of Section 302 of the Act as well as to effectuate what we

believe to be Congress' intent — to have senior officers certify that required material nonfinancial information, as well as financial information, is included in an issuer's quarterly and annual reports. Under this interpretation, we maintain the preexisting concept of internal controls without expanding it by relating it to nonfinancial information.

In their final rules, the SEC did not require any particular procedures for conducting the required review of disclosure controls and procedures. However, it did recommend that each issuer create "a committee with responsibility for considering the materiality of information and determining disclosure obligations on a timely basis."

Disclosure Controls and Procedures and Key Controls

As previously mentioned, key controls is an important internal control process. In fact, I have attempted to make the case that it is the best method for the ongoing evaluation of internal controls. In developing the new term "disclosure controls and procedures," the SEC's intent was to develop a broader concept that includes traditional internal control and emphasizes the importance of the controls that a company uses to ensure the disclosure of all material financial and nonfinancial information. The SEC recognizes that internal control is a critical element of any entity's disclosure controls and procedures. A key controls process therefore will play a critical part in ensuring adequate disclosure controls and procedures.

A company's management, under SEC rules, is allowed to make judgments that focus these quarterly evaluations on developments since the most recent evaluation, areas of weakness or continuing concern, or other aspects of disclosure controls and procedures that merit concern. The stated objective of such a quarterly evaluation of a company's disclosure controls and procedures is for company management to be able to opine on the overall effectiveness of their disclosure controls and procedures. Moreover, I believe the best manner in which a company can accomplish this review is by developing a key controls process. The significant events and judgments reporting process will also play a critical role in assisting with the identification of potential financial and nonfinancial disclosures as will an enterprise risk assessment and management process.

Risk of Nondisclosure and Materiality

In financial reporting, the risk that must be mitigated by disclosure controls and procedures is that material information would not be adequately disclosed to the people who rely upon the company's financial information. Therefore, the question becomes what is material information?

- Information in financial statements and disclosures should be considered material, regardless of any numerical threshold (please forget the five percent rule), if the information involves an omission or misstatement that, in light of surrounding circumstances, makes it probable that the judgment of a reasonable person relying on the information would be changed or influenced by the omission or misstatement.

- All of the pertinent circumstances around an issue or issues should be considered before determining materiality and inclusion or exclusion from a report.

- For financial omissions, the effect of the items should be considered both singularly and in total.

The above is a somewhat simplistic rule for materiality; however, it will work well for a general understanding. For a detailed understanding, one should consult the SEC's *Staff Accounting Bulletin No. 99.*

Sarbanes-Oxley Act Certification and Disclosure Requirements

Since the SEC developed the term disclosure controls and procedures specifically as a requirement in the Sarbanes-Oxley Act Section 302 certifications, one must review the requirements of these certifications and be familiar with these requirements before beginning to understand how to ensure compliance with these requirements. Below is the current certification format as published with the SEC's final Section 404 rules. The form of the Section 302 certification varies a little based on the form of the registrant. However, for example purposes only, the following format is provided:

I, [identify the certifying individual], certify that:

1. I have reviewed this [specify report] of [identify registrant];

2. Based on my knowledge, this report does not contain any untrue statement of a material fact or omit to state a material fact necessary to make the statements made, in light of the circumstances under which such statements were made, not misleading with respect to the period covered by this report;

3. Based on my knowledge, the financial statements, and other financial information included in this report, fairly present in all material respects the financial condition, results of operations, and cash flows of the registrant as of, and for, the periods presented in this report;

4. The registrant's other certifying officer(s) and I are responsible for establishing and maintaining disclosure controls and procedures (as defined in Exchange Act Rules 13a-15(e) and 15d-15(e)) and internal control over financial reporting (as defined in Exchange Act Rules 13a-15(f) and 15d-15(f)) for the registrant and have:

   (a) Designed such disclosure controls and procedures, or caused such disclosure controls and procedures to be designed under our supervision, to ensure that material information relating to the registrant, including its consolidated subsidiaries, is made known to us by others within those entities, particularly during the period in which this report is being prepared;

(b) Designed such internal control over financial reporting, or caused such internal control over financial reporting to be designed under our supervision, to provide reasonable assurance regarding the reliability of financial reporting and the preparation of financial statements for external purposes in accordance with generally accepted accounting principles;

(c) Evaluated the effectiveness of the registrant's disclosure controls and procedures and presented in this report our conclusions about the effectiveness of the disclosure controls and procedures, as of the end of the period covered by this report based on such evaluation; and

(d) Disclosed in this report any change in the registrant's internal control over financial reporting that occurred during the registrant's most recent fiscal quarter (the registrant's fourth fiscal quarter in the case of an annual report) that has materially affected, or is reasonably likely to materially affect, the registrant's internal control over financial reporting; and

5. The registrant's other certifying officer(s) and I have disclosed, based on our most recent evaluation of internal control over financial reporting, to the registrant's auditors and the audit committee of the registrant's board of directors (or persons performing the equivalent functions):

(a) All significant deficiencies and material weaknesses in the design or operation of internal control over financial reporting which are reasonably likely to adversely affect the registrant's ability to record, process, summarize, and report financial information; and

(b) Any fraud, whether or not material, that involves management or other employees who have a significant role in the registrant's internal control over financial reporting.

Date: ....

_____

[Signature]

[Title]

Under the final rules regarding filing of certifications under Section 302, for most public registrants the new format above became effective for reports filed on or after August 14, 2003. However, the SEC is applying the extended compliance period to portions of the introductory language in paragraph 4 and paragraph 4(b) of the required Section 302 certification. In paragraph 4, the extended compliance period is applied to the portion of the introductory language that refers to the certifying officers' responsibility for establishing and maintaining internal control over financial reporting for the company, and the extended compliance period is applied to all of paragraph 4(b). These portions must be provided in the first annual report that is required to include a management report on internal control over financial reporting and thereafter.

Both the Section 302 and 906 certifications are filed as exhibits to a registrant's quarterly reports. This change was made to make it easier to access the certifications via the SEC's Electronic Data Gathering, Analysis and Retrieval (EDGAR) system.

Under the SEC's rules for the retention of manual signatures, companies must retain for a period of five years an original signature page or other document authenticating the certifying officer's signatures that appear in their electronically filed periodic reports. Moreover, the officers may not for purposes of Section 302 signatures have the certification signed on his or her behalf pursuant to a power of attorney or other conforming authority.

Standard for Disclosure Controls and Procedures

One of the first steps that management should take to begin to ensure compliance with the Sarbanes-Oxley Act Section 302 requirements is to develop and promulgate a standard for management in relation to the requirements placed upon management to ensure adequate disclosure controls and procedures. Remembering that disclosure controls and procedures include internal controls, this standard should therefore include a requirement that management maintain an appropriate system of internal control for their areas of responsibility. Please note that any standard that you adopt should be thoughtfully and thoroughly developed to fit the needs of your company. However, for illustrative purposes only, a sample standard follows:

Sample Standard for Disclosure Controls and Procedures

In support of the company's SEC required reporting, each business unit/function/significant area of responsibility must have adequate disclosure controls and procedures to ensure that for their areas of responsibility:

- The organization is able to timely identify and communicate all significant events, judgments, transactions, and internal control issues that have resulted in a potentially consequential impact upon an SEC registrant's operations or financial results.

- All issues identified are communicated to their business unit controller for follow-up by the financial reporting department in a manner that will enable and ensure a timely determination of whether such events should be disclosed in the company's SEC filings.

- The organization must maintain appropriate books and records that will ensure for each SEC registrant the fair presentation in all material respects of the registrant's financial position and results of operations, and enable the analysis of all issues identified and ensure the timely development of SEC disclosures.

- The organization must maintain on an ongoing basis sufficient, effective disclosure controls and procedures to enable the organization to ensure compliance with all of the Sarbanes-Oxley certification applicable requirements.

The specific disclosure controls and procedures necessary to achieve this standard are dependent upon the specific operations and nature of the business performed by the business unit/function/ significant area of responsibility. However, the greatest disclosure controls and procedures process risk is that a new disclosure area will not be timely identified and reported to the company's financial reporting department. This is because financial reporting must rely on the business experts in each area of the company to identify significant changes, via various processes, and communicate these to them so that they can determine the financial disclosures that may be needed. Therefore, the disclosure controls and procedures developed must be adequate to identify and timely communicate to financial reporting any new issues that potentially require disclosure in addition to being able to provide updates for known disclosure areas.

Types of Disclosure Controls and Procedures

Although companies will have many different types of disclosure controls and procedures, primary among these is the system of internal control. Beyond the system of internal control, most companies will probably have three types of disclosure controls and procedures that we will discuss. The first type is a disclosure checklist; the second is a system of supporting certifications; and the third is a disclosure committee.

Disclosure Checklists and Questionnaires

Disclosure checklists and questionnaires can take various forms. They can be manual checklists or automated information systems with built-in alerts. However, the basic principle should be to ensure a positive confirmation to a list of questions that if properly designed would identify most potential areas of financial and nonfinancial disclosure for your company. It is critical that the right personnel prepare, review, and approve the disclosure checklists. Additionally, no matter what questions are asked and how complete the coverage, it is recommended that two additional questions be added. First, a request to disclose anything else that may need to be disclosed even though it was not specifically requested. Second, a request should be made to update the financial reporting department as soon as possible if any significant information becomes known subsequent to the completion of the questionnaire. For example, here are two sample questions:

1. To the best of your knowledge, have there been any other events or transactions that had or could have a consequential impact on the results of operations, financial condition, or cash flows of the company or on any existing or potential financial or nonfinancial disclosure for the current quarter that have not been disclosed?

2. Do you agree to provide, as soon as possible, any information that comes to your attention subsequent to the completion of this disclosure checklist that had or could have a consequential impact on the results of operations, financial condition, or cash flows or on any existing or potential financial or nonfinancial disclosure of the company to be reported for the current quarter?

To develop a disclosure checklist, you would first want to develop questions that relate directly to any significant change in accounting principles and estimates. You would also want to inquire about prior period adjustments, potential lawsuit settlements, divestitures or acquisitions, or any other general financial or nonfinancial area or disclosure that could be impacted over time. You would next want to walk through your income statement, balance sheet, and cash flows statements and determine specific events and judgments related to these areas that may occur and need to be disclosed. Of course, you would want to review the latest registrant Form 10-K, Form 10-Q, and any Form 8-K's to determine additional areas that should be covered.

From the areas identified, you would need to develop a concise set of questions and determine the right personnel to complete, review, and approve the disclosure checklist. Now all you have to do is to ensure that everyone who assists in its completion takes the checklist seriously — very seriously. You should also review the checklist and enhance it as appropriate every quarter.

In completing the disclosure checklist, each business unit/function manager/controller should ensure that, when the disclosure checklist is completed for his or her areas of responsibility:

- Sufficient competent personnel are assigned to complete the disclosure checklists.

- The business unit/function manager/controller responsible for the area completing the disclosure checklist has an adequate review process to support his or her required sign-off on the adequacy of the disclosure checklist's completion.

    - Such review process should include sufficient discussion with key personnel to confirm the adequacy of the disclosure checklist's completion.

    - Adequate review by senior area personnel with supporting certifications of the adequacy of the completion of the disclosure checklist's completion, as appropriate.

Risks of Nondisclosure of Material Financial and Nonfinancial Information

This chapter began with a quote by General Patton, "A pint of sweat saves a gallon of blood." Like all controls, disclosure controls should be evaluated based on a cost benefit analysis. However, the risks of nondisclosure of material financial and nonfinancial information are significant. As already stated in Chapter 2, the Sarbanes-Oxley Act increased the penalties for securities acts violations:

- An individual who engages in a willful violation faces up to a $5 million fine (up from $1 million) and imprisonment for not more than 20 years (up from 10 years).

- The fine for entities that willfully violate the Exchange Act was increased to $25 million (up from $2.5 million).

(The above was adapted from the Lord Bissell book *Client Alert Sarbanes-Oxley Act of 2002.*)

The SEC stated the following in its final Sarbanes-Oxley Act Section 302 rules related to the liability of company principle executive and financial officers:

> An issuer's principal executive and financial officers already are responsible as signatories for the issuer's disclosures under the Exchange Act liability provisions and can be liable for material misstatements or omissions under general antifraud standards and under our authority to seek redress against those who cause or aid or abet securities law violations. An officer providing a false certification potentially could be subject to Commission action for violating Section 13(a) or 15(d) of the Exchange Act and to both Commission and private actions for violating Section 10(b) of the Exchange Act and Exchange Act Rule 10b-5.

However, loss of faith by the investment and financing community due to a failure in your disclosure controls and procedures could be the most costly mistake your company ever makes. Therefore, in the case of disclosure controls and procedures, I suggest you take General Patton's advice and err on the side of conservatism.

Disclosure Checklist Versus the Significant Events and Judgments and Enterprise Risk Assessment and Management Processes

You may be wondering how the significant events and judgments process and an enterprise risk assessment process interface with a disclosure checklist process. Or why a disclosure checklist is needed when you have these other two processes. The value added by a disclosure checklist process is that it is a positive confirmation that ensures the information determined by these other processes is reported timely to those who need to know so that they can review it for possible disclosure.

The significant events and judgments process is based on a concept that one should report what one's boss should know about based on what is taking or has taken place within one's areas of responsibility. No specific areas are required to be reported; therefore, the process produces only negative assurance. In other words, if there are no reported items, then it is assumed that nothing has occurred. However, this conclusion may be erroneous. Items that need to be disclosed may have been overlooked or incorrectly evaluated and considered to not need to be reported. Secondly, although a significant events and judgments reporting process can be successfully implemented throughout the enterprise, there is no assurance that items that are correctly reported to the boss will then be reported to the financial reporting department. This is why a disclosure checklist is also needed.

Similarly, an enterprise risk assessment and management process by itself does not ensure appropriate identification and communication on a timely basis of disclosure items. However, when you combine the significant events and judgments process and the enterprise risk assessment and management process together with a disclosures checklist process, you have a pretty good disclosure process.

Supporting Certification Process

Above, we detailed the actual requirements of the Sarbanes-Oxley Act Section 302 required certifications. Most companies will want to develop a supporting system of certifications. These certifications should:

1. Be based on the signatory's areas of responsibility and knowledge.
2. Be tied directly to the Sarbanes-Oxley Act Section 302 certification statements as directly as appropriate.

For example, you may ask a corporate officer to review and sign off on the entire quarterly or annual report for your company. However, a corporate officer below the principle executive and financial officers is not responsible for the entire company. Therefore, his or her supporting certification should be limited to those areas for which he or she is directly responsible. Secondly, his or her supporting certification should be limited to his or her knowledge. This is where the key controls, significant events and judgments, and enterprise risk assessment and management processes become important. Obviously, an executive can sign anything to the best of their knowledge, because even if they have no knowledge, they can make an honest assertion of agreement to anything to the best of their knowledge. These supporting processes are critical because if they are designed and implemented correctly, they will enable the executive to have the knowledge necessary to be able to give appropriate assurance via a supporting certification to the principle executive and financial officers of the company.

A review of the actual Sarbanes-Oxley Act Section 302 certification statements should be made, and, if a statement is applicable to the supporting signatory, it should be customized to provide the greatest level of assurance that is reasonable under the specific circumstances. The accurate, complete, and timely completion of supporting certifications should be communicated to all involved employees as being a matter of the utmost seriousness. If this message is not delivered directly by the principle executive and financial officers, they should reinforce it.

For the corporate officer's supporting certification process to be able to work efficiently and effectively, the officer must ensure that he or she develops an adequate supporting system of disclosure controls and procedures for his or her areas of responsibility.

- To be able to achieve this objective, the organization's key employees must be fully trained and maintain a reasonable knowledge about the types of financial disclosures that are required of the organization. As noted earlier, this is essential because the primary disclosure risk is that an organization will not identify a new potential disclosure item and communicate it to the financial reporting department so that it can be included in the disclosure review process.

- The organization's key employees must also understand their responsibilities in the disclosure development and review process for their organization.

- There should be an established disclosure development and review schedule for the organization, which fully defines roles and deadlines.

- There should be a process by which the organization's key employees participate in the disclosure development and review processes and then communicate clearly and timely to the corporate officer which disclosures are complete and ready for his or her review and sign-off.

- The corporate officer responsible for signing the Sarbanes-Oxley Supporting Certification should ensure that there is an adequate review process and cascading supporting certifications to support his or her required sign-off.

  - Such review process should include sufficient discussion with key personnel to confirm the adequacy of the documents, disclosures, and filings being reviewed based on their assigned areas of responsibility.

  - Required supporting certifications, as appropriate, to be completed by the area's senior personnel to confirm the adequacy of the documents, disclosures, and filings being reviewed based on their assigned areas of responsibility.

Disclosure Committee

As mentioned previously, the SEC recommended that each issuer create "a committee with responsibility for considering the materiality of information and determining disclosure obligations on a timely basis." This can be a formal committee with a charter, minutes, and all of the other official committee governance requirements, or it can be an informal committee. What is needed is that the right officers of the company review the quarterly or annual report and assert that the financial and nonfinancial disclosures are adequate to ensure compliance with the Securities and Exchange Act rules and the Sarbanes-Oxley Act Section 302 and 906 certifications' requirements.

This is essentially what occurred with the Sarbanes-Oxley supporting certification process. What differs with a disclosure committee is that it should be a forum for the principal executive and financial officers to discuss the SEC filings and ensure that they are comfortable with the adequacy of such. Who needs to attend and how much detail needs to be reviewed at this committee meeting or meetings will depend on what was accomplished via the checklist and supporting certification processes. The better these controls, the less the committee will need to discuss and do.

One should develop disclosure checklists and supporting certification processes as robust as reasonable so as to limit the time and resources necessary to be expended by the disclosure committee. At the very least, a meeting of the right officers with the chief executive and financial officers should probably take place to walk them through the final quarterly or annual report so that they can be comfortable with the document and state that they have reviewed it as required by the Sarbanes-Oxley Act Section 302 certification. The one thing that I would specifically caution against is having only a disclosure committee. Although none of these disclosure controls and procedures are required, the disclosure committee, the disclosure checklists, and the supporting certification processes or some other equivalent processes are needed to effectively mitigate the risk of nondisclosure of financial information.

Planning Review of the Disclosure Controls and Procedures

There should be a quarterly planning review of the disclosure controls and procedures. During the planning review, the actual disclosure controls and procedures should be reviewed and compared to the required assertions. This should include the Sarbanes-Oxley Act Section 302 and 906 certification requirements for which the disclosure controls are intended to ensure appropriate compliance. A thorough review of the disclosure controls and procedures against each assertion should be made and all gaps in control should be identified. For all identified control gaps, an appropriate mitigation plan should be developed. A final planning document should be produced to document the review process, and it should be appropriately reviewed and approved.

Evaluating Disclosure Controls and Procedures

Per the requirements of the Sarbanes-Oxley Act Section 302 certification, the principle executive and financial officers are responsible for establishing and maintaining disclosure controls and procedures. They also are required to evaluate the effectiveness of the issuer's disclosure controls and procedures as of the end of the period covered by the report that is to be issued. A suggested evaluation process for the required evaluation of an entity's disclosure controls and procedures would have three components:

1. During the planning phase each quarter, the disclosure controls and procedures should be reviewed to ensure they will adequately achieve all objectives, including enabling the assurances necessary for the principle executive and financial officers to complete the required certifications.

2. The actual review of the disclosure controls and procedures for the quarter.

    a. As the key controls are reviewed and exceptions are reported for the quarter, the system of internal control will be reviewed. Significant events and judgments will also be reported within the appropriate functions.

    b. The key control certifications, disclosure checklists, and other identified disclosure controls should be received and reviewed by the management responsible for ensuring that they are completed accurately, completely, and timely.

    c. The responsible management should then complete appropriate Sarbanes-Oxley supporting certifications for senior management's reliance. Any exceptions to the supporting certifications should be appropriately resolved.

3. The review of the actual disclosures and SEC filings for the quarter.

The disclosure committee should have access to appropriate documentation showing that all three of these components were adequately completed. The disclosure committee should then review and agree to the conclusions reached about the effectiveness of each registrant's disclosure controls and procedures that will be promulgated in the final SEC filings, and that all other disclosure requirements were achieved.

Disclosure Controls and Procedures Summary

The above discussion is intended to explain how the key controls process should be integrated into the overall disclosure controls and procedures process. It is also intended to give the reader an understanding of the types of disclosure controls and procedures that larger companies will probably implement. However, it is not intended to establish a strict guideline — just a sample framework. Each organization must review its own needs and develop disclosure controls and procedures that will enable it to meet these needs in the most cost efficient and effective manner.

If one develops an enterprise risk assessment and management process, then the company should seek to integrate the disclosure controls and procedures into that process. This would potentially entail transferring the responsibilities for some disclosure controls and procedures to the risk monitoring and management forums and higher-level forums and committees, which would report to both the audit and disclosure committees as appropriate.

CHAPTER 12
DEVELOPING A KEY
CONTROLS SYSTEM

> "An invasion of armies can be resisted,
> but not an idea whose time has come."
> — Victor Hugo

Project Objective

The first step in developing a key controls process is to determine your project's objective. Is the objective simply to build a key controls process that will achieve your Sarbanes-Oxley Act Section 302 and 404 ongoing quarterly and annual management assessment of internal controls requirements? Or do you want to eventually develop key controls for all areas needed to support an overall enterprise conclusion as to the successful achievement of COSO's three objective categories? Do you want to integrate some process reengineering into the project so that you can maximize the project's benefit? Whatever your objective, please remember that a key controls process should always be first and foremost a good management practice. Reengineering, process improvement, cost minimization, and Sarbanes-Oxley Act compliance or any combination of these is the right objective based on what is right for your company. However, no matter what objective you set for this project, please remember that for a key controls process to become an embedded process within your company, it must be based on good management practice. In each step of the project you must help company management to integrate their ideas and enable them to get the maximum benefit out of this process.

A key controls process will enable you to comply with the Sarbanes-Oxley Act's requirements; however, this is the minimum that it can do for your company. Simple compliance should not be the primary objective of a key controls process. The primary objective should be to assist management to better manage their business. When this is the driving principle behind a key controls process, you will find that once company management understands the process, they will be thankful that they have this process.

Management has a need to know that the right things are getting done and that they are getting done right. Management has a need to know and understand the risks that can prevent them from achieving their business objectives. Management needs to know that the judgments that are being made are well founded and reliable. This information and the ability to manage their business better is what a key controls process enables management to accomplish, and it enables them to accomplish it better than they were able to do before. Moreover, the more involved you allow your management team to become in the key controls development process, the better the process will be for your company.

Project Management

There are many sources available to assist you in developing a project plan, time line, identifying resources, and so forth for a key controls development project. Therefore, we will not dwell on these areas. My only suggestion is to ensure that everything you do is coordinated with and agreed to by your external auditor. Second, you should ensure the project has adequate full-time dedicated team members as appropriate.

If you are interested in learning more about how you can be successful in managing a key controls process from the project management skills perspective, I would like to suggest a very good book that a friend of mine wrote: *Getting a Project Done On Time: Managing People, Time, and Results* by Paul B. Williams.

Available Automated Tools

The automated tools or application systems currently available to assist you in developing a key controls process are not that good, to be honest, at least when you compare them to what you would want them to be. The problem with most of these tools is that they were built for another purpose and then were adapted with or without enhancement when the need for Sarbanes-Oxley Act support tools developed. From my own review of the existing automated tools that are currently available, these tools appear to fit into one of four categories:

1. **Risk Assessment Tools** — These tools will generally assist in the identification of the risks in an area and possibly also in the documentation of the mitigation efforts. They may be robust enough to enable an automated risk assessment. The better tools may assist you in developing an ongoing enterprise risk assessment and management process. Based on the tool's risk assessment process, most of these tools can help determine the areas for which you will need to develop key controls in order to support an ongoing Sarbanes-Oxley Act Section 404 and 302 compliance process. Most of these tools can also help you develop the project scope for a process that will support an overall enterprise conclusion as to the successful achievement of one or more of COSO's three objective categories.

2. **Sample Controls Databases** — Most of these tools are an archive of sample process flows, control objectives, sample control activities, and risks. These tools, of course, vary considerably. However, the better tools are actually very good and several are based on best practices — and may even have best practices for your industry. If you can afford these tools, they will be

helpful in decreasing the time and effort required to document process and identify existing controls.

3. **Controls Repositories** — These tools allow you to archive the process flows and control matrices that you develop. The better tools allow you to store the process flow and control matrix files somewhere else and link to these documents. This is especially helpful for policies and procedures, which can change frequently, and linking to these files will allow you to always access the latest versions.

4. **Ongoing Assessment Tools** — These tools allow you to assess your company's internal controls on an ongoing basis. Generally, the assessment process should allow control adequacy conclusions to be determined and documented in the tool. Some of the available tools do not relying on actual testing to support the control adequacy conclusion reached. Nor do they facilitate the linkage to the evidence of control for review and approval. However, the better tools do have these features. The tool will then enable the roll up of these control conclusions for multiple areas so that an overall conclusion for a registrant can be reached and supported. However, none of the tools that I saw support a key controls process. They do not facilitate the usage of minimum standards of control. They do not facilitate the identification and reporting of significant events and judgments, nor any type of integrated risk assessment process.

Of course, the above are actually theoretical classifications. In practice you will find that the available automated tools will be any combination of the above with more or less features from each category. In hopes that if you describe it, they will provide it, I intend to explain what I believe the features would be for the ideal fully integrated key controls automated system.

The Ideal Key Controls Integrated System

What is needed is a fully integrated system that enables the fast implementation of a key controls process. This system would assist in not only the original implementation of a key controls process, but also in the quick development of key controls processes for new acquisitions. The following basis elements would need to be present in this fully integrated system:

1. The system would need to facilitate the quick determination of the scope of the areas to be reviewed and for which key control processes would need to be developed. This should include the ability to define a scope for both a limited project intended only to ensure compliance with Sarbanes-Oxley Act Section 404 and 302 requirements, and a project intended to support an overall enterprise assertion as to the successful achievement of COSO's three objective categories.

2. This system would provide industry specific best practice based process flows and control matrices. The system would facilitate the quick and easy updating of these generic forms into final finished products that would support the adequacy of overall internal control design and

the adequacy of the internal control evaluation system. The system would facilitate the decentralized maintenance of these files with appropriate access control rules and a calendar based work flow process to facilitate the review and approval of updates. This would also include documenting effective dated change history and version control. One should also be able to rollup and report and analyze control activities from multiple perspectives such as: business process, financial cycle, financial account, and application system.

3. This system would facilitate the easy development of key controls and minimum standards of controls based on industry best practices. These systems would also have an integrated testing methodology, and it would be easy to develop a test plan for each key control. Once key controls and testing plans were established, the system would facilitate the monthly review process of validating key controls against minimum standards of control. The system would also link the testing results to the actual evidence of control for easy access, review, and storage. Certifications of key controls would be developed automatically upon completion and approval of the key controls testing, and any key control exceptions would be automatically integrated into the certifications. Significant events and judgments would be an integrated required component of the automated certification process. The automated certification process would also have required fields for all key control exceptions and significant events and judgments in order to ensure these were completed correctly. Work flow processes would facilitate the automated delivery of completed certifications along with any key control exceptions and significant events and judgments to both the direct report's manager and multiple matrix managers as needed. The system would also produce automated summarized certification reports from multiple areas of responsibility, which would be automatically delivered via work flow to each level of responsible management and to the members of the area's risk monitoring and management forum.

4. The system would facilitate the timely completion of the risk monitoring and management forum's responsibilities, including:

   • Enabling the tracking, updating, and status reporting of all identified key control exceptions for each level of responsible management via an online real-time process.

   • Enabling the development and decentralized management of an audit universe and the scheduling of key control process reviews for the forum's areas of responsibility.

   • Enabling the tracking, updating, and status reporting of the internal control documentation supporting the established key controls evaluation process.

   • Enable review of the control environment for the risk monitoring and management forum's areas of responsibility. This would require the ability to develop appropriate evidence of control and linkages into the repository system.

- Enable the review of and assessment of overall risks within the risk monitoring and management forum's areas of responsibility.

- Enable the determination of and tracking of the top tier risks for their areas of responsibility, along with required action plans and parties.

- Enable change management and version control for all processes, along with the ability to ensure appropriate safeguarding of information assets, segregation of duties, and accountability via security access controls and audit trails. The system should facilitate both ad hoc and monthly reporting. Additionally, the system should facilitate the ability to define critical items for which real-time alerts could be established.

- The system should facilitate access to all risk monitoring and management forum information for review by higher-level committees such as a corporate level risk monitoring and management committee and the audit committee.

- The system should also facilitate the easy summarization of all issues and the reporting of appropriate issues to the corporate level risk monitoring and management committee and the audit committee.

CHAPTER 13
NEGATIVE COMPETITION

> **"Facts do not cease to exist because they are ignored."**
> **— Aldous Huxley**

Negative Competition

Every organization has internal control failures, but catastrophic failures hurt everyone involved and must be prevented. A Ford Pinto automobile exploding during rear-end collisions is an example of a catastrophic internal control failure. Not just the physically injured and their families, but Ford's management, employees, stockholders, and almost everyone else were injured parties.

Now you are probably wondering how this was an internal control failure. From a key controls perspective, management establishes systems of internal control to detect and prevent unwanted events. Certainly, the decision to not include a part, which would have prevented these explosions, was an event Ford senior management would have wanted to detect and prevent. However, the system of internal control failed Ford senior management with notorious results.

We have all seen vivid examples of this type of company debacle, many of them on television shows like *60 Minutes*. However, what leads a manager to undercut product quality or safety in order to increase profits? Is it greed? A bad childhood? Or is it something much more endemic to capitalism. Are managers driven by the forces of capitalism to make poor choices? I believe that it is time to admit that Adam Smith's invisible hand can be as dangerous as it can be beneficial, and to actually create internal control systems that can identify and limit this danger.

Both management and the internal audit function evaluate the system of internal control established by management and should be able to detect and prevent these events. However, management and internal auditors are not armed with the tools they need to identify and prevent the weaknesses that lead to these types of debacles. To properly arm management and internal auditors, we need to define a new class of internal control system failure — negative competitive practices.

To enable management and internal auditors to identify negative competitive practices, we need to determine and explain how and why these failures occur so management and internal auditors will be able to search for, detect, and prevent them. We also need to create new requirements to ensure these reviews take place. The enhancement of internal control systems to enable them to identify and prevent negative competitive practices is an expensive public good; therefore, a legislative mandate may be required. However, I believe many management teams will — after reading the rest of this chapter — better understand the risks inherent in their industries and willingly choose this path.

The Two Sides of Adam Smith's Invisible Hand

Adam Smith, in his 1776 treatise, *The Wealth of Nations,* promulgated the theory of laissez-faire, which states that if men are unrestricted and allowed to pursue their own selfish ends, they will be guided by market forces to benefit society. These market forces are supposed to guide them to this end like a benevolent invisible hand. In Smith's famous example, nail factory management were led by unrestricted market forces to specialize their labor, which resulted in the most efficient production methods and produced the greatest output at the most competitive prices. However, capitalistic competitive pressure viewed from the perspective of possible outcomes on society actually includes both positive and negative forces and results. While the positive pressures are well known and named, we will name the negative forces of capitalistic competition — negative competition.

Negative competition can allow, if not force, Adam Smith's nail factory management to artificially restrain prices in order to drive competitors out of business and achieve monopoly profits. Negative competition can allow or force nail factory management to produce knowingly defective or dangerous nails. These nails look like the better quality nails produced by other factories, so factory management can and will price these nails like the better quality nails. When these nails cause serious injuries and deaths, management can settle the lawsuits "out-of-court" using nondisclosure agreements to hide the truth for as long as possible. This invisible negative force can cause factory management to dispose of production waste in mountain streams while spewing tons of dangerous silt into our air. Negative competition can cause factory management to allocate cost from commercial orders to government cost-plus-basis contracts. Or, this invisible negative force can cause factory management to sell more nails than are needed, at much higher prices, causing inefficient income redistribution and defrauding purchasers. This last outcome may seem harmless compared to the others. However, consider the type of frauds that have occurred, such as insurance agents selling the elderly new policies with less coverage in order to generate new commissions. To be more specific, how would you feel if you found a stockbroker churning your grandmother's retirement account in order to earn higher commissions? Or, even worse, doctors imprisoning healthy patients in mental institutions in order to bill millions of dollars in unnecessary medical services? It becomes easy to see how this area can affect us. The point here is that negative competition can allow and/or force management to make decisions that are not in the best interest of society. Worse, negative competition can produce outcomes that are catastrophic in their negative effect on company management, employees, stockholders, and society.

Negative Competitive Practices

The above are all examples of negative competitive practices, which are the direct result of negative competition. Negative competition is simply the negative competitive force component of capitalism.

Just as leverage can have great positive effects on profits, it can have equally negative and destructive effects. Moreover, capitalistic competitive pressures can be equally negative and destructive. There is nothing that intrinsically divides capitalistic forces into positive and negative forces. Only when we review the results of capitalistic competition — the competitive practices against the overall good or bad effect these practices have on society — can we identify these practices as negative. However, it is true that when these practices see "the light of day," it is apparent to all that they are negative practices and should be prevented. To explain the quote in Chapter 2, in modern English what Tartuffe the Imposter said in the famous play by Moliere was, "The public scandal is the crime, sins sinned in private are not sins at all." Unfortunately, far too often this is the view that management and employees use to rationalize their usage of negative competitive practices.

Negative competitive practices occur because full market disclosure of all pertinent information regarding product quality and cost is not possible. Full disclosure is not possible due to the complexity of the processes and markets that produce these goods and services. How many of us would have purchased a Ford Pinto over the other available automobiles if we had known that Ford had left out a relatively inexpensive part that would potentially allow the Pinto to explode during rear end collisions? Clearly, the automobile was overvalued in the marketplace based on its perceived value versus its intrinsic or real value. Its real value is what someone would have been willing to pay for the Pinto given knowledge of the defect. But, of course, consumers did not know about this design flaw. Consumers were not able to know because very large, complex, and dynamic processes and systems inside large corporations like Ford build automobiles. Hundreds if not thousands of people are involved who make literally millions of decisions. Based on this infrastructure, the consumer cannot know what he or she is purchasing. Consumers must trust that the government has developed adequate laws, regulations, and enforcement. And, that the company's management has developed adequate systems of internal control to protect them. But if this is true and this infrastructure of protection is both in place and adequate, then why do so many negative competitive practices occur? The answer is obvious. This infrastructure is in place, but it is inadequate to meet the challenge. There is neither adequate detection nor punishment to prevent some managers from adopting negative competitive practices.

Negative Competitive Practices and the Control Environment

In COSO's *Internal Control - Integrated Framework*, it is the "control environment" that is responsible for setting the "tone at the top" of the organization. This tone is supposed to flow down from the board of directors, guiding the actions of all employees to ensure integrity and ethical values. The control environment and the tone it establishes is the foundation of internal control for the organization providing its discipline and structure. Moreover, it is the integrity of management upon which reliable financial reporting is dependent. Without management integrity, there is no reliability.

If one were to identify the root cause of the recent accounting frauds at companies such as Enron, WorldCom, and HealthSouth, I believe one would find that it was the integrity of management or lack thereof that is the essential element in the internal control structures that was lacking, and which ultimately led to the disintegration of the reliability of these organizations' financial reporting. When challenged with actual financial results that are not comparable to desired financial results, management has a decision to make. They can fairly present their financial position, or they can falsify their financial position and financial reporting in hopes that they will be able to turn the company's actual financial results around before they are caught. When management chooses to falsify their financial results rather than tell the truth, they are utilizing a negative competitive practice (false reporting) because they have succumbed to negative competitive pressure.

One of the key concepts of the COSO definition of internal control is the simple reality that people affect internal control. Internal control is not merely policy manuals and forms, but people at every level of an organization. Moreover, internal control is directly dependent on the integrity and ethical values of these people, and it is most susceptible to their weaknesses. An organization's management can override internal control. An organization's internal control can also be overridden by the collusion of one or more employees. Bottom line — internal control is dependent upon the integrity and ethical values of the organization's management and employees.

The success of an external audit is also directly and absolutely dependent upon the integrity and ethical values of the organization's management and employees. Audit is by its very nature a limited check because only a sample of items is reviewed. Audit conclusions are determined based on this limited sampling that is then applied to the population. Management and employees who are knowledgeable about this intrinsic weakness of an audit approach can use collusion and/or management override to manipulate the system and mislead the auditors into believing an untrue financial position. The reason that management and/or employees would do this is because they have succumbed to negative competition.

Management and employees can succumb to negative competitive pressures at all levels of the organization and cause internal control to fail. This is why the control environment is critical to the long-term survival of an organization. The "tone at the top" must be pervasive and emanate downward throughout the entity to protect it from negative competitive practices.

Management's Adoption of Negative Competitive Practices

Why, generally, would an organization's management risk adopting negative competitive practices? There are several probable scenarios in which they might make this choice:

- The most obvious reason management implements a negative competitive practice is to gain an unfair competitive advantage. This advantage is unfair because market inefficiencies are used to hide differences between market known and management known/actual product qualities or company financial position.

- In another probable scenario, if production flaws exist, management may consider it more cost effective to accept the flaws than to accept the cost to fix them. The potential costs based on product failures, customer dissatisfaction, and possible injuries are considered less costly by management than admitting to production flaws, problems, or errors to internal and/or external customers.

- In another probable scenario, where direct competitors have adopted negative competitive practices and quality differences between products cannot be efficiently promulgated and reflected in market prices, management may feel forced to adopt similar practices to prevent a competitive disadvantage.

All of these probable scenarios are enabled by market failures to price goods and services correctly. They are all caused by a lack of management integrity and ethical values.

Inadequate Corrective Controls

Obviously, the Enron type of negative competitive practice as affected by senior company management who succumb to negative competitive pressures has had a severe negative effect on our financial markets and society. I would say, however, that all forms of negative competitive practices are bad. Even though there are penalties for companies and employees who succumb to negative competition, these penalties are generally inadequate. Usually, there is only a chance perpetrators will get caught. They are generally only caught in the most severe cases and years can go by before some cases are brought to trial. By then, cases that would have been difficult to prove become nearly impossible, and the resulting financial penalties and unfavorable publicity are generally not in the best interest of society.

Financial penalties can result in inefficient income redistribution. For example, management at a theme park fails to properly maintain a thrill ride. Several people are injured, or worse yet, killed. As we all know, lawsuits resulting from situations like this are usually settled for millions of dollars. These dollars come out of the pockets of all of us. The settlements are paid directly by increased prices for the goods and services of the theme park or indirectly through the insurance company settlement, which is paid from our insurance premiums. Unfavorable publicity and financial penalties injure both the guilty and the innocent. They destroy companies, employees, and jobs. Unfortunately, the people injured or killed by the negative competitive practices are generally not restored. The result can be inefficient income redistribution when the injured parties are killed, because it is the relatives, not the direct victims, who end up reaping the benefits of these million-dollar settlements. Society ends up indirectly taxed to create millionaires out of a few who are unworthy except for the fact that their relative paid the ultimate price. This process is sort of like a lottery we are all forced to play, but no one should want to win.

Prior to the Sarbanes-Oxley Act, the emphasis was placed on reforming the civil tort system to address these problems. This resulted primarily from the large number of significant negative competitive practices and their resultant inefficient income redistribution. From a societal perspective, however, our objective should not be to reform the civil tort system so that injured people recover less to reduce this inefficient income redistribution. The objective should be to prevent the occurrence of the events that resulted in these tort cases in the first place. Preventing the occurrence of these events (i.e., negative competitive practices) will reduce the burden on society not only in monetary terms, but also in terms of human suffering. We need to develop internal control systems that include key controls that will be able to detect and prevent the occurrence of many negative competitive practices. This is in everyone's best interest — especially management's.

Current Preventative and Detective Controls

So, what are the current preventative and detective controls present in most major corporations? The business ethics of company management and the systems of internal control they establish are the primary detective and preventative controls over the use of negative competitive practices. All scenarios that result in significant negative competitive practices appear to require inefficient and ineffective market communication and weak management business ethics. For employees or lower-level management to be responsible for significant negative competitive practices there must also be a weak internal control structure. The adoption of negative competitive practices is inherent in capitalism. With complex processes and markets responsible for producing, pricing, and selling products there are always inefficiencies that can be exploited, and in a capitalistic system, sound business ethics are generally no match against a competitive advantage. Since it is inadequate to punish the guilty, the structure supporting business ethics and systems of internal control must be strengthened to ensure negative competitive practices cannot be used to achieve unfair competitive advantages.

Enhancing Preventative and Detective Controls

The framework necessary to enhance the review of internal control structures already exists. In 1992, COSO issued *Internal Control - Integrated Framework*, or the COSO framework, which we have already explained in this text. Within the auditing profession, this framework established **management's integrity** as the foundation of the system of internal control. This was a watershed development in the theory of auditing because it forced a profession focused on identifying so-called "hard controls" to recognize that it is the "soft controls" that are the most important. These soft controls must be reviewed. However, as we all should know from a litany of recent financial reporting debacles at Enron, WorldCom, and HealthSouth, those in management who were responsible for ensuring sound business ethics failed.

Negative Competition and Key Controls

As explained earlier, it is the control environment that is most important in preventing negative competition. However, as we learned in Chapter 8, key controls assist us the least in reviewing this component of internal control. Still, I believe the Sarbanes-Oxley Act has presented management with the mandate needed to encourage them to learn how to control negative competition. I do not doubt that it will take extensive development of tools, procedures, and people. However, let's reminisce about the development of external auditing and some of its initial failures. Most of the external audit profession's generally accepted auditing standards were developed through trial and error — usually through significant errors in financial statements that were not discovered using the current standards of review. For instance, the reason we audit all sites with significant inventory at the same time is because someone perpetrated a major inventory overstatement (fraud) simply by moving inventory between sites. Developing procedures to identify and prevent negative competition will take time and tribulation, but the end will ensure it was worth the effort.

An Enhanced Mandate for Internal Control

Internal controls can never provide absolute assurance that negative competitive practices will not occur. There is always the risk of management override of the internal control system, or collusion between employees. Internal controls can only provide reasonable assurance that negative competitive practices will not occur based on the cost/benefit decisions made by management in determining the level of audit review and internal control to apply. But given the Sarbanes-Oxley Act legislative mandate, as key controls processes are implemented and other audit procedures are enhanced, the internal control systems reviewed will be improved.

What I propose is that the current Exchange Act requirements should eventually be enhanced to include:

- A quarterly requirement for public companies to both ensure and assert that their system of internal control provides reasonable assurance that significant negative competitive practices would be prevented or detected on a timely basis.

- A quarterly requirement for public companies to disclose any negative competitive practices to the registrant's external auditors and audit committee of the board of directors.

- An annual requirement for public companies to obtain a review of their system of internal control so that this system can be independently certified as adequate to provide reasonable assurance that significant negative competitive practices would be prevented or detected on a timely basis. Both the registrant's management and their independent auditor would be required to state that the registrant's system of internal control was inadequate to prevent or detect significant competitive practices should one be found to exist.

Consider the significance of these enhancements. An unfavorable opinion on the appropriateness of a registrant's internal control system's ability to detect and prevent significant negative competitive practices should have enough impact in financial markets to ensure they rarely occur. Unfavorable opinions would support consumer lawsuits, while unjustly accused managements could use favorable opinions in their support. Every member of our society will benefit. First, we will have safer, better quality goods and services. Second, a structure will exist to enforce and ensure stronger business ethics.

CHAPTER 14
KEY CONTROLS INTEGRATED
FRAMEWORK

> **"There are risks and costs to a program of action.**
> **But they are far less than the long-range risks**
> **and costs of comfortable inaction."**
> **— John F. Kennedy**

Key Controls Integrated Framework

In the previous chapters, we discussed all of the components of a key controls integrated framework. It is now time to discuss how one should probably approach the development of this framework.

Step One — Policy Development

Assuming that you will adopt the theoretical framework explained in this text thus far, the first step to developing a key controls process should be to develop appropriate policies. There are several written policies that each company should consider developing:

- **Management's Responsibilities for Internal Control** — This policy should state clearly the responsibilities of internal audit, board members, the audit committee, the disclosure committee, and company management for ensuring an effective system of internal control. The policy should also establish the responsibility for ensuring an effective "tone at the top" in compliance with the COSO objectives. These responsibilities are discussed in COSO's *Internal Control - Integrated Framework's* Executive Summary (which is available online at www.coso.org). Such a policy would probably need to be reviewed and approved by the board of directors.

- **Key Controls Process and Responsibilities** — This policy should clearly define the key controls process, state the goals of the process, and define the specific roles and responsibilities for each level that assists in the process. A corporate level policy may be necessary along with a supporting procedure for each significant area of responsibility.

- **Disclosure Controls and Procedures and Responsibilities** — This policy should state clearly the responsibility of management to ensure that they maintain adequate disclosure controls and procedures for their areas of responsibility.

- **Enterprise Risk Assessment and Management** — This policy should state clearly the roles and responsibilities of the members of the risk-monitoring forums and how these forums operate with the higher-level committees and the audit committee.

Step Two — Key Control Process Development

For most companies, due to the immediate need to satisfy Sarbanes-Oxley requirements, a key controls process should first be developed for all of internal control over financial reporting. This key controls process should be developed based on the development process detailed in Chapters 3 through 8, and should include an integrated significant events and judgments reporting process. Since one many eventually want to develop key controls for all key business processes, the key controls development project should be based on an appropriate approach that can be expanded to include all key business processes. Since key controls include internal controls within all three of the COSO control objective categories, an approach that documents internal control processes is probably preferable because of its expandability across the enterprise. An approach based on financial cycles or significant accounts would be difficult to expand across the enterprise.

If one begins the development of their key controls process by identifying and documenting all the enterprise's business processes that include internal control over financial reporting or other disclosure controls and procedures, they should be able to identify all the business processes that will need to be reviewed to achieve Sarbanes-Oxley requirements. However, as I stated previously, on an ongoing *quarterly* basis, public registrants will need to ensure that they are able to review their disclosure controls and procedures and ensure that these controls are effective. Therefore, one should not only consider what is required to satisfy the Sarbanes-Oxley Section 404 requirements, but should consider what is required to achieve all Sarbanes-Oxley Section 302, 906, and 404 requirements on an ongoing basis in defining the scope of their key controls development project.

It is important to understand that the control activities within these business processes that we will review, document, and test for adequacy of design will probably be a larger set of control activities than those that we will test in detail to ensure the effective operation of internal control. This is true when defining the controls to test for an ongoing monthly key controls process and when defining the controls to test for an annual Sarbanes-Oxley Section 404 evaluation of internal control over financial reporting. To be efficient, however, the controls that are documented and reviewed for design adequacy must satisfy both of these criteria.

As the PCAOB stated in their proposed audit standard: "The proposed standard would require that the auditor obtain evidence about the operating effectiveness of internal control over financial reporting for all relevant assertions for all significant accounts and disclosures." Therefore, I would suggest two more detailed reviews should probably be performed to assist in ensuring adequate identification of the key business processes that will need to be reviewed to enable Sarbanes-Oxley Section 404 compliance. First, a review of account balances; second, a review of financial disclosures. However, as in any case involving Sarbanes-Oxley Section 404 compliance, the advice of one's external auditor should be obtained and considered.

Review of Significant Accounts

For each registrant, an analysis of the income statement and balance sheet accounts can be used to determine the company processes and automated systems that are responsible for creating the significant account balances. The level of account summary that should be reviewed to ensure this exercise is effective will vary. Each registrant will need to be reviewed to determine the appropriate summary level for significant accounts that will need to be reviewed in order to determine the company processes and automated systems responsible for generating the transactions of which the account balance is composed.

Review of Financial Disclosures

A review of the latest annual Form 10-K and quarterly Form 10-Q filings for each registrant will determine the population of disclosures that will need to be reviewed. For each disclosure, the company area or areas responsible for developing the disclosure should be determined. Any significant automated systems that support these disclosures should also be identified. These areas and systems, along with those explained in Chapter 11, and the processes and automated systems identified above in the review of significant accounts should include most of the company's disclosure controls and procedures.

Since you will probably not be able to develop key controls for all desired areas by the initial filing of your company's first Section 404 compliant internal control report of management, I would suggest that you approach the development of key controls for all areas that directly relate to the achievement of the financial control assertions first. Areas identified as key business processes for which key controls are not developed should then have appropriate COSO-based self-assessment certifications developed.

Self-assessment Certifications

As one develops a key controls process, one will probably need to utilize self-assessment certifications. These certifications should be based on COSO's objective categories. I would anticipate that the surveys would be utilized for areas where key controls have not yet been developed. At first, these surveys may need to be used to ensure appropriate review of the control environment. However, the goal should be to replace self-assessment certifications as soon as possible with key controls processes for all areas for which key controls will be developed. On an ongoing basis it may be prudent to maintain the usage of self-assessment certifications for all internal control not included within the key controls process. These self-assessments, along with the key control processes, would then give management support that their overall internal control processes are effectively operating as designed.

Project Scope and Materiality

When determining the areas within a registrant's disclosure controls and procedures and internal control over financial reporting that will need to be reviewed, there is a tendency to want to use materiality to eliminate areas that are clearly immaterial. While this is reasonable, it is somewhat dangerous if done incorrectly. One must remember that materiality is applied both per item and in total. A number of excluded items may be immaterial individually, but the risk is that when reviewed as a whole along with other areas that were potentially missed, the combined total could be material and lead to an ineffective management review. This should, of course, be avoided. Therefore, I suggest that only entire entities such as divisions, companies, or subsidiaries be excluded on the basis of being immaterial, since all account balances and disclosures for these areas should be able to be uniquely identified and reviewed. One should avoid, for example, the exclusion based on materiality of account balances, processes, areas, and disclosures that are part of an entity or service company — unless one is certain that the ending account balances related to the area, along with all other excluded areas, and areas that were potentially not identified and missed, will be immaterial.

Step Three — Development of an Enterprise Risk Assessment and Management Process

Once key controls processes are in place for most of the company's disclosure controls and procedures, including the internal control over financial reporting key business processes, it is time to incorporate the review of these key controls into an overall enterprise risk assessment and management process. This integration should eventually eliminate the need to utilize self-assessment certifications for all areas that have implemented key controls and enterprise risk assessment and management processes. The control environment reviews, as performed by the risk-monitoring forums, should enable this achievement.

The company will hopefully recognize the value of a key controls process as these processes are developed for each business area. Once management fully realizes the value of these management practices, it is anticipated that key controls processes and enterprise risk assessment and management will be adopted and implemented company wide.

The Changing Role of Internal Audit

As you have developed key controls processes and integrated them into an enterprise risk assessment and management process, the role of internal audit has evolved. Internal audit's traditional role was to review the company's system of internal control. The key controls and enterprise assessment processes have incorporated many of the practices of internal audit. However, internal auditors will continue to play a vital role for the company — they will be the ones who ensure that the key controls and enterprise risk assessment and management processes are operating as designed.

Additionally, when major process changes occur within the company, internal audit resources will probably still be required to ensure the key controls and enterprise risk assessment and management processes are updated appropriately. Most importantly, although the processes described within this text will definitely cover the COSO control objectives related to reliability of financial reporting, the company will still need assurance that the objectives in the other two categories of effectiveness and efficiency of operations and compliance with laws and regulations are achieved. Therefore, although the methods employed by internal audit to review these areas will change, the need will endure, as will their role in providing assurance over internal control, risk management, and governance processes.

A Final Word

In this book, the author has attempted to explain how to build the best key controls process possible. However, the author is limited in his knowledge and experience in this new area — as is everyone. Therefore, the reader should understand that although the author's advice is the best he was capable of giving, internal control processes are unique to the company for which they are designed. Although many rules were explained, nothing in this text should be taken as legal advice. Further, the author does not make any guarantees that following any advice presented in this text will work in all situations, and the reader must adjust all of the advice given to the specific circumstances inherent in his or her company(s).